IHAANAH

DR TAMIM ZUBAIR

To Ammi and Abba

What I am today is because of you.

Contents

Preface   *vii*

Acknowledgements   *ix*

Author   *xi*

1. Munharif   1

2. Urooj-o-Zawaal   11

3. Bad-Unwani   30

4. Aghaaz-e-Ikhtitaam   73

5. Anjaam-e-Qaaynaat   103

6. Zuhoor-e-Ummat   116

Bonus   125

Jazaak Allah   129

Preface

"O Allah, I seek refuge in You from the accursed Satan, from his madness, his pride,and his poetry"

"IHAANAH" is an Arabic word that means "disrespect", and this book explores the striking contrast between two groups of people in the modern world—those who, despite having incomplete or misinterpreted knowledge of their religion, hold a strong belief in their cause, live with a clear purpose, and have ultimately conquered the world; and Muslims, who possess the perfect and complete guidance of Islam, yet remain in a state of heedlessness for over a century.

On one hand, these goal-driven people dedicate their entire lives to their religion, land, and ideological narratives, passing down the same purpose to their children. No matter where they are in the world, their commitment remains unwavering, and their collective efforts shape global affairs. On the other hand, Muslims, despite having the ultimate truth about this world and the Hereafter, have become lost—waking up each day only to consume fake news, believing the false portrayal of their own faith, fearing the idea of an Islamic state, and considering Ilm-e-Deen as backward and outdated knowledge.

Instead of seeking knowledge, strengthening their faith, and instilling Islamic values in their families, Muslims have become aimless, disconnected from their Deen, and distanced from their true purpose. This state of self-imposed ignorance and neglect is what justifies the title of this book—"IHAANAH", a reflection of the profound disrespect we, as an Ummah, have shown towards the divine knowledge, legacy, responsibilities and deen entrusted to us.

Acknowledgements

In the Name of Allah the Most Compassionate, Most Merciful.

All praise is for Allah Lord of all worlds.

The Most Compassionate, Most Merciful.

Master of the Day of Judgment.

YOU ALONE WE WORSHIP and YOU ALONE WE ASK FOR HELP.

Guide us along the Straight Path.

The Path of those You have blessed not those You are displeased with, or those who are astray.

(Al Fatiha)

Author

My name is Muhammad Tamim Zubair Ansari and I live in Lucknow, India. I am a 20 year old currently in the 2nd year of Bachelors in Dental Surgery with my roots in the historic town of Kalpi. My journey has been one of transformation; one that began with little understanding of Deen or knowledge but has now brought me to a place of awareness, purpose, and devotion.

There was a time when I was distant from the teachings of Islam and unaware of the depth of its wisdom. But as I grew, I realized the immense beauty and responsibility of living a life guided by the Quran and Sunnah. This awakening changed everything for me. It reshaped my goals, my priorities, and my outlook on life.

I initially aspired to be a profound oncosurgeon, striving for excellence in my medical career. However, as I witnessed the struggles of the Ummah, I felt a calling far greater than personal ambition. I decided to dedicate my life to serving the Ummah through knowledge, education, and action.

"I did not create jinn and humans except to worship Me. (Quran 51:56)"

My life now revolves around learning and teaching, both in my professional field and beyond. I am committed to fostering meaningful discussions about faith, science, and the pressing issues of our time. I believe that transformation begins within, and my goal is to inspire others to seek truth, reflect deeply, and work toward the betterment of themselves and the community.

"He is the One Who created death and life in order to test which of you is best in deeds. And He is the Almighty, All-Forgiving. (Quran 67:2)"

I see every moment as an opportunity to grow closer to Allah and to contribute to the unity, strength, and progress of our people.

CHAPTER I

Munharif

THE GOLDEN ISLAM

Aariz ibn Zubair was a devout Muslim living in Baghdad during the flourishing period of the Abbasid Caliphate, a time known for its intellectual and cultural advancement. From an early age, he was immersed in the teachings of Islam. His father, a businessman, was a pious man who would always prioritize his religious duties, ensuring that his family was committed to the daily practices of Islam.

Aariz was taught the pillars of Islam by his father, including regular prayers (Salah), fasting in Ramadan(Sawm), giving charity (Zakat), and the importance of pilgrimage (Hajj). He was not only taught these practices, but their significance in shaping a moral and just life was instilled in him from a young age. His father would remind him that worship (Ibadah) was not just confined to prayer but included every action performed with good intention, whether it was work, charity, or family obligations.

As Aariz grew, he became increasingly devoted to knowledge. He would attend the madrasas (Islamic schools) in the heart of Baghdad, where scholars taught not only the Quran and Hadith but also subjects like jurisprudence (Fiqh), Arabic grammar, philosophy, and science. Aariz engaged in debates and discussions with learned scholars from diverse backgrounds, strengthening his understanding of both religious and secular knowledge.

Aariz was deeply inspired by the works of famous scholars of the time, including Imam Malik and Imam Shafi'i, whose teachings on Islamic jurisprudence shaped his daily life. He also believed in the importance of studying Islamic history and the lives of the Sahabah (companions of Prophet Muhammad PBUH) to draw lessons for contemporary challenges.

Aariz was not just a student of knowledge but also a teacher and mentor. He believed strongly in the transmission of knowledge to future generations. In his home, he created a small study circle for the children of his neighborhood. His teaching methodology focused on practical application of knowledge, ensuring his students understood the relevance of their studies in the real world. He would teach them not only the Quranic verses but also how to apply the teachings in daily life, whether in interactions with others, trade, or dealing with personal struggles.

He emphasized the importance of the five daily prayers, and every child in his circle would be taught to pray at the age of seven, with a focus on the spiritual benefits of each prayer and its connection to one's relationship with Allah.

Aariz was particularly concerned with the moral upbringing of his children. He would tell them stories from the life of the Prophet Muhammad (PBUH) and his companions, particularly focusing on patience, humility, and honesty, teaching his children to strive for these qualities in their own lives.

His approach to family life was deeply rooted in Islamic principles. His wife, Aisha, was a strong partner in raising their children, and together they prioritized both religious education and practical skills. They would ensure their children knew the value of earning an honest living, often bringing them along when they would visit the markets or engage in trade to teach them about the ethics of business and honesty in transactions.

He made sure his children were not only well-versed in religious knowledge but were also given the opportunity to pursue secular education. He believed that a well-rounded education was important for living in a complex world. As a result, his children were taught both Islamic sciences and mathematics, astronomy, and medicine, which were flourishing subjects during the Abbasid period.

He would emphasize the importance of community, encouraging his children to interact with their neighbors, both Muslims and non-Muslims, with respect and kindness, reflecting the Islamic values of peace and tolerance.

His life was a reflection of the principles of Islam, devotion to worship, pursuit of knowledge, and service to the community. He died at a relatively young age, but his children continued his work, becoming scholars, teachers, and community leaders in Baghdad.

The lessons he imparted to his children and students carried on through generations, contributing to the legacy of Islamic scholarship and piety that thrived during the Abbasid Caliphate. His life remains a model of how to balance religious devotion with intellectual growth, while also teaching the next generation to serve both their faith and society.

THE NEW ISLAM

Aariz lives a busy life, juggling work, social commitments, and personal pursuits. He grew up in a Muslim family and was taught the basics of Islam as a child. He knows how to pray and has memorized a few surahs of the Quran, but religion is not a priority for him anymore. It exists in his life more as a cultural identity than as a way of life. He rarely prays. He tells himself he is too busy or tired and that Allah is forgiving, so missing prayers won't matter much. Jumu'ah is the only prayer he occasionally attends, more out of habit or family pressure than genuine devotion. During Ramadan, he fasts because it is expected of him. However, the spiritual essence of fasting, self-control, gratitude, and mindfulness of Allah, feels distant to him. For him, it is more about following tradition than seeking spiritual growth. He owns a Quran, but it sits on a shelf, untouched for months. He doesn't read or reflect on its teachings, and his understanding of Islam remains shallow, limited to what he learned as a child.

In his pursuit of a modern, fast-paced lifestyle, he is deeply indulged in practices that Islam prohibits, often ignoring the consequences. He spends hours binge-watching TV shows and movies that promote un-Islamic values. Music with explicit content dominates his playlist, and he frequently scrolls through social media, consuming content that distracts him from remembering Allah. He works in a corporate job that involves dealings with interest (riba), despite knowing that it is prohibited in Islam. He justifies it by saying, "It's impossible to survive without it in today's world." He is in casual relationships with his colleagues and ignores the boundaries set by Islam. Night outings, parties, and extravagant spending have become a regular part of his life, leaving little room for reflection on his actions. He hardly gives Zakat or engages in charity, believing that his taxes and occasional donations are enough. He spends lavishly on luxuries but feels no urgency to fulfill his religious obligations.

> *"Narrated Abu Hurairah (ra) The Prophet (peace be upon him) said: Certainly a time will come when people will not bother to know from where they earned the money, by lawful means or unlawful means. (Sahih al Bukhari 2083)"*

He rarely spends quality time with his parents, who long for his company and advice. While he provides financial support, he is emotionally distant, often brushing off their reminders to pray or reflect on Allah. If he has children, he prioritizes their secular education and extracurricular activities but neglects their Islamic upbringing. He assumes they will learn about Islam on their own someday, just as he did, and doesn't see it as his responsibility.

He prioritizes wealth, career, and status over spiritual growth. His pursuit of worldly success leaves little time for faith, has never sought deeper knowledge of Islam and views it as "too difficult" or "incompatible" with modern life, feels the need to conform to societal norms and fears being judged as "too religious." He prioritizes acceptance from others over his relationship with Allah. He is consumed by his daily routine and rarely reflects on his purpose in life or the meaning of his existence.

THE ZION LIFE

Benjamin Cohen is a Zionist who adheres to a radical interpretation of his nationalist ideology. He believes in the superiority of his people and justifies extreme measures, including violence, to achieve what he considers the divine right to exclusive control over the land. He interprets religious texts selectively to justify his belief in the superiority of his group. He views other groups, particularly Muslims and Polytheists, as obstacles to his people's destiny and supports their displacement and oppression as a necessary step toward fulfilling his ideological goals. He strongly supports the use of force to expand territorial control, endorsing military actions, demolitions, and even collective punishment. He believes in maintaining a constant state of power and intimidation to suppress opposition. He frequently engages in spreading propaganda that dehumanizes others, uses platforms, from public speeches to social media, to perpetuate hatred and instill fear. He supports policies and practices that marginalize and oppress communities he perceives as threats. He actively participates in campaigns advocating for restrictive laws, land confiscation, and other measures that harm minorities. He shows little regard for the suffering of others, dismissing their struggles as irrelevant or justified by his cause.

From an early age, Benjamin instills a sense of superiority in his children. He teaches them to view others as inferior and unworthy of compassion. He encourages his children to participate in youth programs that emphasize militarism, self-defense, and loyalty to the cause. These programs often glorify violence and reinforce a sense of enmity toward perceived opponents. He teaches his children a biased version of history, portraying his group as perpetual victims and others as perpetual aggressors, reinforcing a sense of entitlement and resentment. He participates in rallies, meetings, and campaigns that promote aggressive policies. He is often seen as a leader in pushing for actions that further marginalize and harm others, opposes any peace initiatives or attempts at coexistence, viewing them as threats to his goals. He dismisses negotiations as futile and advocates for absolute dominance.

ANALYSIS

The life sketches presented highlight a profound regression in the Muslim Ummah over the last century. The first sketch paints a vivid picture of the life of an average Muslim during the Abbasid Caliphate, an era often regarded as the golden age of Islamic civilization. It illustrates how every aspect of his life, be it relationships, services, or even the upbringing of his children, was deeply intertwined with his faith. His existence revolved around Islam, and his ultimate purpose was to attain closeness to Allah. Every act, whether private or public, was a means to fulfill this higher spiritual objective.

In contrast, the second sketch unveils the modern Muslim's life, a life detached from its spiritual roots. Islam, for him, is no longer a comprehensive way of life but rather a set of cultural practices passed down generationally. The Qur'an, once a source of guidance and reflection, is now read merely as a childhood ritual. Obligatory acts like Jumu'ah prayer and fasting during Ramadan are observed, not out of conviction or submission to Allah, but to conform to societal expectations. His aspirations are rooted in materialism, his sole preoccupation is the pursuit of wealth, and he fails to impart any meaningful Islamic education to his children. Stripped of purpose, his life is a hollow chase for worldly success, far removed from the divine calling of La ilaha illallah.

The third sketch offers a sobering glimpse into the mindset of a typical Zionist. Here lies an individual whose every thought and action are meticulously aligned with a grand vision, world domination to pave the way for the arrival of their so-called Messiah (Dajjal). Mentally and physically prepared, they work tirelessly to fulfill their objectives, employing every available means to assert their influence. This relentless dedication starkly contrasts with the modern Muslim's complacency. It is a painful irony that while the Zionist thrives on strategy, ambition, and preparedness, the average Muslim today has little to no understanding of the very declaration of faith that forms the cornerstone of Islam.

Since the establishment of Israel in 1948, the Zionist agenda has unfolded with precision, leaving no stone unturned in its quest for global dominance. They have successfully infiltrated the most powerful nations, such as the United States and the United Kingdom, by holding their assets hostage through an intricate financial web. Institutions like the Federal Reserve, the World Bank, and major asset management companies like Vanguard and BlackRock are under their influence, enabling them to dictate global economic policies. Their dominance extends far beyond banking, they control vital sectors such as healthcare, pharmaceuticals, entertainment, media, arms trade, and even the global gold and currency markets.

This control is not merely coincidental; it is a calculated effort rooted in their eschatological beliefs. For them, these efforts are essential steps in preparing for the arrival of their Messiah (Dajjal). By monopolizing resources and controlling narratives, they aim to solidify their hegemony and suppress any opposition, particularly from Muslims.

The juxtaposition of these three sketches serves as a stark wake-up call for the Ummah. The Zionists are fully mobilized, employing a multi-dimensional strategy that encompasses political, economic, cultural, and ideological spheres. Meanwhile, the Muslim Ummah, once a beacon of knowledge and leadership, finds itself in a state of dormancy. The last century has witnessed the steady decline of Islamic civilization, riddled with disunity, intellectual stagnation, and spiritual detachment. This decline has allowed adversaries to exploit the void and establish their dominance.

In subsequent chapters, we will delve deeper into the historical timeline of this decline, contrasting it with the meteoric rise of Zionist influence. From the dismantling of the Ottoman Caliphate to the occupation of Palestine and the institutionalization of apartheid in Israel, we will analyze the systematic erosion of the Muslim Ummah's power. We will also explore how Zionist strategies, including control over key industries and manipulation of global policies, have positioned them as leaders of the modern world. Only by understanding these dynamics can we begin to chart a course toward the revival of the Muslim Ummah.

> *"Anas bin Malik narrated that the Messenger of Allah(peace be upon him) said: There shall come upon the people a time in which the one who is patient upon his religion will be like the one holding onto a burning ember. (Jami' at Tirmidhi 2260)"*

CHAPTER II

Urooj-o-Zawaal

THE RISE OF JEWS

The Jewish community's rise to prominence over the last century as influential leaders in various fields and as a globally recognized community can be attributed to a combination of strategic efforts.

Education

Jewish culture historically values education and intellectual development. The Talmud encourages the pursuit of knowledge as a religious obligation, leading to a high level of literacy and intellectual achievement within Jewish communities. Many Jews pursued advanced degrees in science, medicine, law, and the arts. Today, Jews are disproportionately represented among Nobel Prize winners, accounting for over 20% despite being less than 0.2% of the world population.

Economy

Jews have often been excluded from land ownership and certain professions throughout history. This led them to adapt by excelling in trade, finance, and other specialized fields. Over time, Jews became prominent in banking and financial industries, especially in Europe and later in the United States. Families like the Rothschilds played pivotal roles in shaping global dominance. Many Jews started small businesses, which later grew into multinational corporations. This adaptability helped them gain economic power.

Solidarity

Jews developed a strong global network due to their widespread population all over the world. This enabled them to support one another economically, politically, and socially. Jewish communities often established organizations to assist fellow Jews, such as educational scholarships, financial assistance, and social welfare programs. Jewish philanthropists have contributed heavily to education, research, and cultural institutions, further enhancing their community's influence.

Media

Many of the early pioneers of Hollywood, such as Louis B. Mayer (MGM) and the Warner brothers, were Jewish immigrants. They built an industry that continues to shape global culture and public opinion. Jews have had significant roles in major media outlets, allowing them to influence narratives and public perceptions.

Polity

In the late 19th and early 20th centuries, Theodor Herzl and other leaders advocated for a Jewish homeland, culminating in the creation of Israel in 1948. Organizations like the American Israel Public Affairs Committee (AIPAC) and other Jewish advocacy groups have built significant influence in Western politics, particularly in the United States. The Holocaust generated global sympathy for the Jewish people, leading to stronger support for Israel and Jewish causes worldwide.

Establishment of Israel (1948)

Israel was established in a geopolitically significant region, providing economic and military advantages. With substantial financial and military aid from the U.S. and other Western nations, Israel built one of the most advanced militaries in the world. Israel is a leader in technology and innovation, with many startups and advancements in fields like cybersecurity, medicine, and agriculture.

External Support

The Jewish community, particularly in the United States, has been instrumental in securing financial, political, and military support for Israel. After World War II, many Jews in Europe benefited from U.S. led reconstruction programs, allowing them to rebuild their lives and businesses. Nations like the U.S. welcomed Jewish immigrants, many of whom became influential in shaping American society.

Culture

Jewish communities have a deep sense of identity and resilience, shaped by historical persecution and shared religious practices. Jews have adapted to changing circumstances throughout history, allowing them to thrive even in challenging environments. Despite assimilation pressures, Jewish traditions and values have been preserved through religious practices and cultural institutions.

Innovations

Jews have made groundbreaking contributions in various fields, from Albert Einstein in physics to Sergey Brin (co-founder of Google) in technology. Jewish scientists and doctors have pioneered advancements in medical research and innovation.

Victimhood

The atrocities of the Holocaust became a focal point for global advocacy, gaining Jews significant political and moral support. It was used as a rallying point for the establishment and support of Israel. The Jewish community has effectively utilized the media to highlight their struggles and successes, shaping public opinion in their favor.

THE FALL OF MUSLIMS

"Hudhaifah bin Al-Yaman narrated that the Prophet (peace be upon him) said: "By the One in Whose Hand is my soul! Either you command good and forbid evil, or Allah will soon send upon you a punishment from Him, then you will call upon Him, but He will not respond to you. (Jami' at Tirmidhi 2169)"

The decline or "sleeping" state of the Muslim Ummah over the past century can be concluded in the following heads.

Division

European colonization dismantled the Ottoman Caliphate in 1924 and divided the Muslim world into artificial nation-states, weakening the concept of unity (One Ummah). Internal divisions between Sunni, Shia, and other sects have caused conflict and disunity, diverting focus from collective progress. The rise of nationalism replaced the idea of a unified Ummah, with Muslims prioritizing national interests over collective Islamic identity.

No Leadership

After the abolition of the Ottoman Caliphate, no central leadership emerged to unite and represent the Ummah. Many Muslim-majority countries are ruled by authoritarian regimes that prioritize their power over the welfare of the people, leading to oppression and stagnation. Many Muslim nations have relied on Western powers for political, economic, and military support, leading to a lack of independence and exploitation.

Intellectual Decline

The Islamic golden age emphasized both religious and worldly knowledge. In recent centuries, this balance has been lost, with many Muslims neglecting scientific, technological, and philosophical advancements. Colonization disrupted traditional Islamic education systems and replaced them with Western-style curricula, often alienating Muslims from their religious heritage. Intellectuals from Muslim-majority countries often migrate to the West due to a lack of opportunities, depriving their nations of talent and innovation.

Dependency

Muslim-majority countries are rich in resources like oil and gas, yet external powers and corrupt elites have exploited these resources, leaving the masses impoverished. Widespread poverty and economic mismanagement have prevented many Muslims from accessing basic necessities and opportunities for development.

Deviation

Many Muslims have become overly influenced by Western materialism, prioritizing wealth and status over spirituality and Islamic values. A lack of understanding and practice of the core teachings of Islam has led to moral and spiritual decline and the introduction of non-Islamic practices into religion has diluted the purity of Islamic teachings.

Political Instability

Western interventions (e.g., in Iraq, Afghanistan, and Palestine) have destabilized many Muslim-majority regions, causing immense suffering and displacement. Regional powers often engage in proxy wars, further weakening the Ummah (e.g., Saudi-Iran rivalry, Syrian conflict). The establishment of Israel in 1948 and the ongoing oppression of Palestinians have symbolized the inability of the Ummah to protect its people and lands.

Media and Propaganda

Western media portrays Islam and Muslims negatively, leading to a lack of confidence and pride in Islamic identity. Hollywood and Western media dominate global culture, eroding traditional Islamic values and promoting secular lifestyles.

Decline in Social Responsibility

Muslims have become less proactive in spreading the message of Islam and engaging with non-Muslim communities and have become self centered, focusing on individual success rather than collective progress.

ANALYSIS

Over the centuries, Muslims have gradually weakened, largely due to their detachment from faith and an increasing obsession with materialism, wealth, and conformity to modern societal narratives. While once a people of intellectual, spiritual, and economic strength, Muslims have now become fragmented, losing sight of their collective purpose.

In contrast, the Jewish community—despite being a global minority of around 15 million people—has remained resilient, united, and deeply connected to its faith, education, and economic growth. Their focus on self-preservation, financial strength, religious teachings, and intellectual progress has allowed them to wield significant influence across multiple domains, including economics, politics, and academia. Meanwhile, Muslims, despite being over 1.9 billion strong, remain deeply divided—split into sects, ethnicities, castes, and nationalities. Today, a Muslim may not even know the name of his next-door neighbor, let alone feel any true connection to the global ummah.

The strength of any community lies in unity and purpose. A united people remain unshaken by external influences, whereas a divided people are easily manipulated, distracted, and ultimately derailed from their true mission in life. Jewish children across the world are raised to read, write, and understand Hebrew—the language of their scriptures. This religious literacy fosters a deep connection to their history, traditions, and faith, reinforcing their collective identity. Meanwhile, Muslim children, even in devout households, often grow up memorizing nursery rhymes like"Twinkle Twinkle Little

Star" instead of the Quran and Sunnah. Parents today consider it a success if their children can speak English fluently, but fail to ensure they understand even the basics of Arabic—the language of the Quran.

This shift in priorities is not accidental but rather a direct result of systematic conditioning. A friend of mine once remarked that governments and global powers do not perceive Muslims as a threat, not because of their size, but because they no longer fit into the framework of higher policies and global influence. In other words, Muslims today are seen as passive contributors to the economy, rather than intellectual competitors or global decision-makers. They wake up, work, earn, eat, sleep, and repeat—living in a cycle of survival, rather than a mission of revival.

The Jewish texts contain fragmented, altered, and often historically inaccurate information—yet the Jewish people follow them with unwavering dedication. Despite the ambiguities and contradictions in their scriptures, they preserve their language, practice their rituals, and apply their teachings in everyday life. On the other hand, Islam is the only divine religion whose scripture, the Quran, remains 100% authentic, unchanged, and perfect, containing accurate knowledge of the past, present, and future. It provides guidance on science, politics, economics, ethics, human nature, and even the unseen realities of the hereafter—yet Muslims, despite having access to this divine knowledge, have abandoned it. Instead of living by the Quran and Sunnah, we have outsourced our thinking to secular ideologies, chasing after awed modern systems while neglecting the comprehensive wisdom of Islam. This tragic negligence has reversed our roles in history—the people with falsehood lead, while the people with truth remain lost, divided, and powerless.

Historically, Muslims were world leaders, scholars, scientists, inventors, and investors—driving innovation and shaping civilization. Today, many are reduced to daily wage laborers, struggling for survival, completely detached from their intellectual and spiritual heritage. The question we must ask is: How did we allow this to happen? And more importantly, how can we reclaim our lost legacy?

> *"Narrated Anas: Allah's Messenger (peace be upon him) said, "From among the portents of the Hour are (the following): -1. Religious knowledge will be taken away (by the death of Religious learned men). -2. (Religious) ignorance will prevail. -3. Drinking of Alcoholic drinks (will be very common). -4. There will be prevalence of open illegal sexual intercourse. (Sahih Al Bukhari 80)"*

If we search a little bit about the great scholars and thinkers in Islam, the list never ends.

Al-Khwarizmi (780–850)

Field: Mathematics, Astronomy, Geography.

Often called the"father of algebra," Al-Khwarizmi wrote the influential book Al-Kitab al-Mukhtasar Hisab al-Jabr w'al-Muqabala ("The Compendious

Book on Calculation by Completion and Balancing"), from which the term algebra is derived. He introduced the concept of algorithms, which is essential in computing. He made significant contributions to the development of trigonometry and improved the accuracy of astrolabe and astronomical tables.

Ibn al-Haytham (965–1040) Field: Optics, Physics, Astronomy.

Known as the"father of optics," Ibn al-Haytham developed the theory of vision, light, and color. He proved that light travels in straight lines and reflected on surfaces. His Book of Optics (Kitab al-Manazir) laid the groundwork for modern optical science and influenced the development of lenses and microscopes. He pioneered the scientific method and was a precursor to experimental physics.

Ibn Sina (980–1037)

Field: Medicine, Philosophy, Chemistry.

Ibn Sina is often referred to as the"father of modern medicine." His medical encyclopedia, The Canon of Medicine, was a standard reference in Europe and the Islamic world for centuries. He also contributed significantly to philosophy, logic, and metaphysics, particularly through his works on Aristotelianism. He made advancements in the understanding of diseases, pharmacology, and surgical procedures.

Al-Razi (865–925)

Field: Medicine, Chemistry, Philosophy.

Al-Razi, also known as Rhazes in the West, is considered one of the greatest early chemists. He was one of the first to distinguish between smallpox and measles. He wrote the Kitab al-Hawi, an encyclopedia of medicine that introduced many surgical techniques and treatments. He is credited with pioneering the use of alcohol as an antiseptic and was one of the earliest to use sulfuric acid in laboratory experiments.

Ibn al-Nas (1213–1288)

Field: Medicine, Anatomy.

Ibn al-Nas is known for discovering the pulmonary circulation of blood. He was the first to describe the circulatory system in a way that would later influence modern physiology. He also contributed significantly to medical knowledge in areas such as physiology, anatomy, and pharmacology.

Al-Zahrawi (936–1013)

Field: Medicine, Surgery.

Known as the"father of modern surgery," Al-Zahrawi wrote Al-Tasrif, a 30-volume medical encyclopedia, which became the standard reference in Europe for many centuries. He invented and refined numerous surgical instruments, including forceps, scalpels, and catheters. He is credited with introducing new techniques in the fields of dentistry, obstetrics, and surgery.

Al-Biruni (973–1050)

Field: Astronomy, Geography, Mathematics, Physics.

Al-Biruni made significant contributions to the study of astronomy and was among the first to calculate the radius of the Earth. He also made advancements in the measurement of time and the study of the motion of celestial bodies. His work in geography and trigonometry helped shape modern map-making and spatial analysis.

Ibn Battuta (1304–1369)

Field: Geography, Travel, Anthropology.

Ibn Battuta was a renowned explorer who traveled over 75,000 miles across Africa, Europe, Asia, and the Middle East, documenting his extensive journeys in his travelogue, Rihla ("The Journey"). His observations contributed greatly to geographical knowledge of the 14th century and provided insights into the diverse cultures he encountered.

Jabir ibn Hayyan (721–815)

Field: Chemistry, Alchemy, Medicine.

Often referred to as the"father of chemistry," Jabir ibn Hayyan was one of the first to propose the idea that chemistry could be a systematic science based on experimentation. He wrote extensively on alchemy and was credited with inventing many chemical processes, such as distillation, crystallization, and filtration. His work laid the foundation for modern chemistry.

Nasir al-Din al-Tusi (1201–1274)

Field: Astronomy, Mathematics, Philosophy

Al-Tusi was a leading figure in astronomy and is known for his contributions to the development of the Tusi couple, an astronomical model that influenced later models of planetary motion. He contributed to trigonometry and geometry, developing a mathematical model that helped improve the accuracy of astronomical observations.

Al-Kindi (801–873)

Field: Philosophy, Mathematics, Optics, Music.

Known as the"Philosopher of the Arabs," Al-Kindi made significant contributions to philosophy, particularly in the areas of logic, metaphysics, and ethics. He also worked on mathematics and astronomy, particularly in improving the accuracy of astronomical tables. Al-Kindi was one of the first to introduce the concept of cryptography to the Islamic world.

Banu Musa Brothers (9th Century)

Field: Engineering, Mathematics.

The Banu Musa brothers, Muhammad, Ahmad, and al-Hasan, made notable contributions to engineering and mathematics, particularly in automata (mechanical devices). They wrote the influential book Kitab al-Hiyal (The Book of Ingenious Devices), which contains designs for various mechanical devices and automata that were centuries ahead of their time.

Khalid ibn Yazid (670–704)

Field: Chemistry, Alchemy.

He is considered one of the earliest Muslim alchemists and is credited with spreading the science of alchemy in the Islamic world. Khalid ibn Yazid is often associated with the development of the art of distillation and purification of substances.

Salahuddin Ayyubi (1137–1193)

Recaptured Jerusalem from the Crusaders in 1187 after the Battle of Hattin. Unified Muslim forces in Egypt, Syria, and Iraq. Known for his chivalry and fair treatment of both Muslims and non-Muslims.

Osman I (1258–1326) – Founder of the Ottoman Empire

Established the Ottoman dynasty, which lasted over 600 years. Unified Turkish tribes under Islamic rule.

Mehmed II (1432–1481) – The Conqueror of Constantinople

Captured Constantinople in 1453, marking the end of the Byzantine Empire. Transformed the city into the new Ottoman capital, Istanbul. Promoted science, education, and religious tolerance.

Suleiman the Magnificent (1494–1566)

Expanded the Ottoman Empire to its peak, including parts of Europe, Africa, and the Middle East. Strengthened Islamic law and governance. Patronized architecture, literature, and arts.

Babur (1483–1530) – Founder of the Mughal Empire

Established Mughal rule in India after the Battle of Panipat (1526). Promoted Persian and Islamic culture in South Asia.

Aurangzeb (1618–1707)

Expanded the Mughal Empire to its greatest territorial extent. Implemented strict Islamic law and governance. Promoted the construction of mosques and Islamic education.

Shah Abbas I (1571–1629) – Safavid Empire

Strengthened the Persian Safavid Empire and made it a global power. Developed Isfahan into a major center of Islamic art and culture.

Tipu Sultan (1751–1799) – The Tiger of Mysore

Fought against British colonial rule in India. Developed advanced military tactics and rocketry.

Sultan Abdul Hamid II (1842–1918) – The Last Powerful Ottoman Caliph

Resisted European colonial influence in the Muslim world. Initiated the Hijaz Railway to connect Muslims to Makkah and Madinah. Promoted Islamic unity and opposed Zionist plans in Palestine.

Muhammad Iqbal (1877–1938) – Philosopher and Political Leader

Advocated for an independent Muslim state, leading to the creation of Pakistan. Revived the concept of Islamic self-determination through poetry and philosophy.

King Faisal of Saudi Arabia (1906–1975)

Modernized Saudi Arabia's economy and infrastructure. Strengthened Islamic unity and supported the Palestinian cause.

Dr. Israr Ahmed (1932–2010) – Islamic Scholar and Thinker

Founded Tanzeem-e-Islami, an Islamic revivalist movement focusing on the establishment of a just Islamic system. Dedicated his life to reviving the Qur'anic teachings and spreading awareness about the political and economic system of Islam. Delivered thousands of lectures on Islam, history, and the decline of the Muslim Ummah, emphasizing the need for unity and spiritual revival. Strongly opposed Western secular influence in Muslim societies and called for a return to Quranic governance.

Mufti Tariq Masood (Born 1975) – Contemporary Islamic Scholar and Speaker

A leading scholar, known for his practical approach to Islamic teachings in modern times. Addresses contemporary issues, including family life, social justice, financial matters, and youth challenges. Advocates for Islamic unity while providing deep insights into religious and societal concerns.

Maulana Ilyas Kandhlawi (1885–1944) – Founder of Tablighi Jamaat

Founded Tablighi Jamaat in 1926 as a grassroots movement to revive Islamic spirituality and practice among common Muslims. Focused on self-reformation, Dawah (Islamic preaching), and reviving Sunnah, emphasizing simplicity and personal piety. His movement rapidly spread across South Asia and later the world, influencing millions to return to basic Islamic principles. Advocated non-political engagement and peaceful propagation of Islam, making the Tablighi Jamaat one of the largest Islamic movements globally.

Maulana Syed Abul A'la Maududi (1903–1979) – Islamic Thinker and Political Leader

Founded Jamaat-e-Islami in 1941, advocating for the establishment of an Islamic state governed by Shariah. Wrote extensively on Islam, governance, and modernity, producing influential works like "Tafhim-ul-Quran"and "The Islamic Way of Life." Opposed secularism and Western ideologies, arguing that Islam provides a comprehensive political, economic, and social system. Played a major role in Islamic revivalism, influencing modern Islamist movements worldwide. Strongly criticized un-Islamic political systems and worked towards integrating Islam into contemporary governance models.

Mohammed Hijab (Born 1991)

A well-known Muslim debater, apologist, and public speaker who actively engages in interfaith dialogues and debates, particularly against atheists, Christians, and secularists. Holds multiple academic degrees, including a Master's in Islamic Studies and Applied Theology, and has contributed to discussions on Islamic philosophy, history, and theology. Known for his powerful rhetoric, logical arguments, and deep understanding of Islamic doctrines, often debating figures such as Jordan Peterson, Douglas Murray, and Christian apologists like David Wood. Has played a key role in defending Islam in Western discourse, particularly through his YouTube platform and public appearances. Strongly advocates for the revival of Islamic identity among Muslims and challenges secular, liberal, and anti-Islamic narratives. Co-founded Sapience Institute, an organization focused on intellectual defense of Islam and Dawah (Islamic outreach).

bad-Unwani

After the fall of the Ottoman Caliphate in 1923, for the first time in centuries, Muslims found themselves leaderless, vulnerable, and fragmented. Sensing this unprecedented weakness, Western powers seized the opportunity to introduce colonial rule, accompanied by widespread propaganda designed to detach Muslims from their faith and principles. The Ottoman era had been a time of global prosperity, intellectual advancements, and military dominance—a period when powerful nations like England and America paid jizya to the Ottomans in hopes of avoiding conquest. Yet, as the West steadily gained strength, they realized that mere military power would never be enough to defeat the Islamic civilization.

Curious about the secrets behind the Ottoman Empire's centuries-long dominance, Western scholars and policymakers studied Islamic scriptures in search of an answer. What they discovered shocked them—they found that Islam offers the most well-structured, just, and successful system of governance, economy, law, and society ever conceived. The Quran and Sunnah laid the foundation for a flourishing, self-sustaining empire, where justice, knowledge, and strategic governance kept the Muslim world at the pinnacle of global influence.

Realizing that they could never subdue Muslims through direct force, Western powers devised a new strategy—one that would weaken Islam from within. Instead of waging a military war, they launched an ideological war, designed to undermine Muslims' confidence in their own faith. They infiltrated Muslim lands with secular ideologies, Western philosophies, and nationalist sentiments, shifting focus from Islam as a comprehensive way of life to a mere set of rituals. They distorted Islamic history, portraying the caliphates as oppressive regimes rather than centers of knowledge, governance, and global leadership. Education systems were redesigned to prioritize Western thought, while Islamic scholarship was sidelined.

They worked tirelessly to separate religion from politics, economy, and governance, making Islam appear irrelevant to modern life. Muslims were taught that Islam is only about personal spirituality and has nothing to do with ruling nations, managing economies, or influencing global affairs. Arabic was systematically removed from education systems, ensuring that future generations would struggle to understand the Quran firsthand. Over time, Muslims began to view their faith as something outdated, something that belonged in mosques but not in the real world.

The West also knew that materialistic people would never resist oppression, so they flooded the Muslim world with distractions—entertainment, consumerism, and an endless pursuit of wealth. Muslims were indoctrinated to believe that power, success, and happiness lie in wealth, luxury, and Western lifestyles, not in faith, family, or community strength. The traditional Islamic economic system, based on justice and fairness, was replaced with capitalism and interest-based banking, ensuring that Muslim nations remained financially dependent on the West.

The culmination of these tactics resulted in the reconstruction and corruption of Islam in the public mind. The West encouraged Muslims to be "religious"—but only within the framework they designed. Today, a Muslim who prays five times a day, fasts in Ramadan, gives charity, and performs Hajj is seen as completely harmless to global powers. This is the Islam they want—one that teaches peace, secularism, and submission in the face of injustice. They want Muslims to believe that turning the other cheek is the ultimate form of piety, that resistance against oppression is extremism, and that striving for an Islamic governance system is a relic of the past. They fear only those few Muslims who truly understand Islam—not just as a spiritual path, but as a complete way of life, encompassing political, economic, and social systems. These are the people they silence, the ones they label as radicals or extremists, because they know that once Muslims return to their fundamental principles, the balance of power will shift once again. Using a series of tactics, they have completely infiltrated our belief.

Step-1

Can't counter through Intellect?

KILL!

When the Jews and Western leaders failed to challenge Muslims intellectually or find inconsistencies in their scriptures, they turned to brutal massacres and systematic oppression to weaken the Muslim world. Throughout history, countless Muslim communities have faced genocide, ethnic cleansing, and unjustified wars, often under fabricated pretexts designed to justify aggression. From the Crusades to colonial-era atrocities, from the mass killings in Palestine to the wars in Iraq, Syria, and Afghanistan, Muslims have repeatedly been targeted, not for any wrongdoing, but simply for their identity and faith.

1948 – Establishment of Israel and the Nakba

In 1948, following the expiration of the British Mandate in Palestine, Israel declared itself an independent state. This event triggered the first Arab-Israeli War as neighboring Arab nations, including Egypt, Jordan, and Syria, opposed the establishment of Israel. The war resulted in the mass displacement of approximately 700,000 Palestinians, an event known as the "Nakba" or "Catastrophe." Many Palestinian villages were systematically depopulated and destroyed, forcing refugees into neighboring countries such as Lebanon, Jordan, and Syria, where many still remain in refugee camps today. This conflict laid the foundation for the ongoing Israeli-Palestinian dispute, with issues of land ownership, refugee rights, and statehood remaining unresolved.

1980–1988 – Iran-Iraq War

The Iran-Iraq War was a devastating conflict between Iran, led by Ayatollah Khomeini, and Iraq, under Saddam Hussein. The war began when Iraq launched an invasion of Iran, seeking to capitalize on Iran's post-revolution instability and assert dominance in the region. The U.S. and other Western nations, fearing the expansion of Iran's revolutionary ideology, supported Iraq with intelligence, military aid, and economic assistance. The war was characterized by brutal trench warfare, chemical weapons attacks (such as Iraq's use of mustard gas), and significant civilian casualties. After eight years of fighting, the war ended in a stalemate, with neither side gaining significant territorial advantage. However, it left both nations economically and socially devastated, further polarizing the Middle East.

2003–2011 – Iraq War

In 2003, the United States, under President George W. Bush, invaded Iraq on the pretext that Saddam Hussein's regime possessed Weapons of Mass Destruction (WMDs) and had ties to terrorist groups like Al-Qa*da. These claims were later proven to be false. The invasion led to the rapid overthrow of Saddam Hussein, but it also resulted in massive instability. The power vacuum left by the collapse of Saddam's government led to widespread sectarian violence between Sunni and Shia groups, as well as insurgencies against the U.S. military presence. In 2011, the U.S. formally withdrew its troops, but Iraq remained unstable, eventually leading to the rise of IS*S in 2014. The war resulted in hundreds of thousands of deaths, large-scale displacement of civilians, and long-term damage to Iraq's infrastructure.

2011–2024 – Syrian Civil War

The Syrian Civil War erupted in 2011 as part of the Arab Spring movement, with protests against President Bashar al-Assad's government escalating into a brutal conflict. The war became increasingly complex as various factions, including the Free Syrian Army, Islamist militant groups, Kurdish forces, and the Assad regime, fought for control. The U.S. became involved by supporting rebel groups and conducting airstrikes against IS*S. Russia and Iran, on the other hand, backed the Assad regime. Over the years, the conflict has led to the deaths of hundreds of thousands and the displacement of millions, making it one of the worst humanitarian crises of the 21st century. Cities like Aleppo and Homs were devastated, finally the rule of al-Assad has been thrown out by Hayat Tahrir al Sham(HTH) under the leadership of Mohammed Abu al-Jolani.

1995 – Srebrenica Massacre

During the Bosnian War, Bosnian Serb forces under General Ratko Mladić carried out the genocide of over 8,000 Bosniak Muslim men and boys in Srebrenica, a U.N.-designated "safe zone." Despite the presence of Dutch U.N.

peacekeepers, the Serb forces overran the town, executing thousands and burying them in mass graves. This massacre is considered the worst atrocity in Europe since World War II and was later ruled as genocide by international courts.

2003–Present – Darfur Conflict in Sudan

The conflict in Darfur, Sudan, began when rebel groups accused the government of marginalizing non-Arab communities. The Sudanese government responded by arming the Janjaweed militia, which carried out widespread atrocities, including mass killings, rape, and displacement of civilians. Hundreds of thousands of Muslims were killed, and millions were displaced, with the violence being labeled as genocide by the International Criminal Court (ICC).

2013 – Rabaa Massacre in Egypt

In August 2013, Egyptian security forces violently dispersed sit-in protests by supporters of ousted President Mohamed Morsi in Cairo's Rabaa al-Adawiya Square. The crackdown resulted in the deaths of over 900 people, marking one of the deadliest mass killings in Egypt's modern history. The event symbolized the return of authoritarian rule under Abdel Fattah el-Sisi, with widespread repression of political dissent.

2014–Present – Uyghur Persecution in China

The Chinese government has been accused of committing human rights abuses against the Uyghur Muslim population in Xinjiang. Reports indicate that over a million Uyghurs have been detained in "re-education camps," where they face forced labor, political indoctrination, and severe restrictions on religious practices. Allegations of forced sterilizations, cultural erasure, and mass surveillance have led to accusations of genocide against China.

2016–Present – Rohingya Crisis in Myanmar

The Rohingya, a Muslim minority in Myanmar, have faced systematic persecution for decades. In 2017, the Myanmar military launched a violent crackdown, leading to mass killings, sexual violence, and the displacement of over 700,000 Rohingya to Bangladesh. The U.N. has described the crisis as a "textbook example of ethnic cleansing."

2019 – Christchurch Mosque Shootings in New Zealand

A far-right extremist carried out a terrorist attack on two mosques in Christchurch, killing 51 Muslim worshippers and injuring dozens more. The attack was livestreamed on social media and highlighted the global risc of Islamophobia and white supremacist extremism.

2020 – Anti-Muslim Violence in India

In 2020, communal violence erupted in Delhi, India, primarily targeting Muslims. Dozens were killed, and numerous homes, businesses, and mosques were set on fire. The violence coincided with protests against a controversial citizenship law that was discriminatory toward Muslims.

The Afghanistan War

The war in Afghanistan has been one of the longest and most devastating conflicts in modern history, spanning multiple decades and involving global superpowers like the Soviet Union and the United States. It has resulted in the deaths of hundreds of thousands of Afghans, the displacement of millions, and the destruction of the country's infrastructure, all while shaping global geopolitics. The war first escalated on a major scale when the Soviet Union invaded in December 1979, attempting to prop up a communist government that was facing resistance from Afghan Mujahideen fighters. The Soviet occupation led to brutal warfare, with over 1 million Afghan civilians killed and nearly 5 million forced to flee as refugees, mostly to Pakistan and Iran. The U.S., Saudi Arabia, and Pakistan supported the Mujahideen with weapons and funding as part of their Cold War strategy to counter Soviet influence. After a decade of resistance, the Soviet forces withdrew in 1989, leaving Afghanistan in political turmoil. After the 9/11 attacks in 2001, the U.S. and its allies invaded Afghanistan, claiming to dismantle Al-Qa*da and remove the Taliban from power. The war resulted in over 200,000 Afghan deaths (including civilians, fighters, and government forces). More than 3 million displaced Afghans. Trillions of dollars spent by the U.S. and NATO.

The Taliban were quickly removed from power, but they launched a prolonged insurgency against U.S.-backed Afghan governments. Over the years, the war became highly unpopular due to corruption in the Afghan government, civilian casualties, and the failure to achieve long-term stability.

1948–Present – Genocide and Apartheid in Israel

The situation in Gaza has reached a catastrophic level, particularly since the most recent intensification of the Israeli-Palestinian conflict. As of recent reports, Israeli military operations in Gaza have led to millions of deaths, primarily among Palestinian civilians, including men, women, and children. According to the United Nations, more than 2,000 Palestinians were killed during the 2014 Gaza War, with over 500 of them being children. More recent flare-ups, including those in May 2021, saw over 250 Palestinian casualties in just a few days, with many of the victims being civilians.

The number of injured civilians is staggering. By 2021, the World Health Organization reported that over 12,000 Palestinians had been injured during escalations, many of whom were severely wounded due to airstrikes, artillery shelling, and ground operations. The injuries often include serious burns, loss of limbs, and internal injuries due to the usc of hcavy artillery and airstrikes on densely populated areas.

The displacement of Palestinian families due to Israeli attacks has reached alarming proportions. In May 2021 alone, more than 100,000 Palestinians were displaced from their homes, fleeing to UN shelters, relatives' homes, or even makeshift tents in Gaza. The situation has left many people with no access to basic necessities like food, clean water, and medical care. According to the United Nations Relief and Works Agency (UNRWA), more than 1.5 million people in Gaza are currently in need of urgent humanitarian assistance, with a significant portion of the population living below the poverty line and experiencing food insecurity.

On September 7th, 2023, the Israeli military escalated its military operations in Gaza, leading to a new wave of violence and destruction that has been described by many human rights organizations and observers as a genocide. This period of intensified conflict was marked by heavy Israeli airstrikes, artillery bombardments, and ground incursions into the Gaza Strip, leaving a devastating toll on Palestinian civilians.

Reports indicate that within the first few weeks, over 1,500 Palestinians were killed, with the majority of casualties being women, children, and elderly people. Human rights groups, including Amnesty International and Human Rights Watch, have raised alarm over the disproportionate use of force, with bombings targeting densely populated civilian areas, hospitals, and schools, in violation of international humanitarian law. Additionally, the extensive use of airstrikes, artillery shells, and drones has led to catastrophic damage to Gaza's infrastructure, further exacerbating the humanitarian crisis.

By the end of September 2023, the number of injured individuals had surged to over 7,000, with many of the wounded suffering from critical injuries, including severe burns, amputations, and traumatic brain injuries. The health system in Gaza, already strained due to the long-standing blockade and previous conflicts, has been overwhelmed by the scale of the casualties, with medical facilities struggling to cope with the massive influx of patients. Many hospitals, which had already been operating under difficult conditions, were severely damaged by airstrikes, further hindering their ability to provide care.

The displacement of Palestinian families reached alarming levels, with more than 500,000 people being forced to flee their homes in just the first month of the conflict. Many sought refuge in UN-run shelters, mosques, and schools, but these places too were often targeted by airstrikes. The displacement has left hundreds of thousands of people without access to clean water, food, or proper sanitation, leading to a further deterioration in living conditions. Many of those displaced were already living in poverty due to the ongoing blockade and previous conflicts, making their survival even more difficult in the aftermath of the 2023 escalation.

The Israeli military's actions, particularly the targeting of civilian infrastructure such as water and electricity plants, homes, schools, and mosques, have contributed to a humanitarian disaster of unprecedented scale. According to the United Nations, over 80% of Gaza's population is in urgent need of humanitarian aid, with many facing food insecurity, malnutrition, and the lack of access to essential services like healthcare and clean water, and around 62,000 people have been killed which includes majority of women and children.

Ben Gurion Canal

The new discoveries of oil and natural gas in the Levant Basin, amounting to 122 trillion cubic feet of natural gas at a net value of $453 billion (in 2017 prices) and 1.7 billion barrels of recoverable oil at a net value of about $71 billion, offer an opportunity to distribute and share a total of about $524 billion among the different parties, in addition to the many intangible but substantive advantages of energy security and cooperation among long-time belligerents.

As Israel continues its onslaught on the besieged Gaza Strip, talks about a long-discussed economic opportunity known as the Ben Gurion Canal Project have surfaced online.

Named after Israel's founding father, David Ben-Gurion, the project, conceived in the late 1960s, sought to create an alternative route to the Suez Canal, the primary shipping route connecting Europe and Asia.

The US had once proposed to use some 520 nuclear bombs on the Negev Desert (Naqab) to help create the canal. With Gaza razed to the ground, there have been alleged plans to literally cut corners and reduce costs by diverting the canal straight through the middle of the Palestinian enclave. However, the presence of Palestinians there would remain an obstacle.

Step-2

Can't suppress through Killing?

DIVIDE!

One of the most significant divisions within Islam is between Sunnis and Shias, which originated from political disagreements over leadership after the passing of Prophet Muhammad(peace be upon him). However, some theories suggest that colonial powers, particularly the British, exploited these differences to weaken Muslim unity. The British, during their rule in India and other Muslim lands, followed a well-known strategy of "divide and rule," often favoring one group over another to create friction. Documents and accounts from the colonial period indicate that British officials encouraged religious disputes in their occupied territories, ensuring that Muslims remained internally divided and unable to form a unified resistance.

Similarly, the rise of Mirza Ghulam Ahmad Qadiani in the late 19th century is viewed by some as an event that further contributed to sectarian fragmentation. Mirza Ghulam Ahmad claimed to be a reformer and later declared himself as a Mahdi and Messiah, a claim that was rejected by mainstream Muslims. Some scholars argue that British authorities, who ruled India at the time, indirectly supported or tolerated his movement because it weakened the broader Islamic resistance against colonial rule. The Ahmadiyya movement, which emerged from his teachings, faced severe opposition from mainstream Muslims, adding to the complexity of sectarian identities in South Asia.

Over time, various other sects and movements emerged, some with seemingly political motivations rather than purely theological ones. Whether these divisions were purely organic or influenced by external manipulation remains a topic of debate. However, what is clear is that sectarian conflicts have significantly weakened Muslim societies, making them easier to control and influence by foreign powers.

> *"Indeed, you O Prophet are not responsible whatsoever for those who have divided their faith and split into sects. Their judgment rests only with Allah. And He will inform them of what they used to do. (Quran 6:159)"*

Sunni Islam

Sunnis make up the majority of Muslims worldwide, and they believe in the leadership of the community through consensus, with the Caliph being a political and religious leader, but not infallible or divinely appointed.

Four Sunni Schools of Jurisprudence

These schools of thought govern Sunni Islamic law and practice:

Hanafi (most widespread, prominent in South Asia, Turkey, and the Balkans)

Maliki (prevalent in North and West Africa)

Shafi'i (common in East Africa, Southeast Asia, and parts of the Arabian Peninsula)

Hanbali (found in parts of the Arabian Peninsula, notably Saudi Arabia)

Shia Islam

Twelver Shia (Imami)

The largest branch of Shia Islam, which believes in a line of 12 Imams starting with Ali ibn Abi Talib, the cousin and son-in-law of Prophet Muhammad (PBUH). The Twelvers consider these Imams to be divinely appointed leaders who possess special spiritual and political authority.

Usuli (dominant within Twelver Shia Islam)

Akhbari (a minority sect that rejects the idea of ijtihad, or independent legal reasoning)

Ismaili Shia

This group believes that the leadership passed to Ali's descendants through his son Ismail. They are split into multiple branches, the largest being the Nizari Ismailis, with the Aga Khan being their spiritual leader.

Zaydi Shia

Predominant in Yemen, Zaydis believe in a different line of succession and leadership based on Ali's descendants, focusing on the leadership of a "just Imam" rather than an unbroken line of 12 Imams.

Sufism (Tasawwuf)

Sufism is a mystical and spiritual dimension of Islam, practiced across both Sunni and Shia communities. Sufis seek a direct personal experience with Allah through rituals, poetry, music, and devotion. While not a sect in the traditional sense, Sufism has often been marginalized or even suppressed by both political and religious authorities at various times in history. Sufi orders (Tariqas) include groups like the Qadiriyya, Naqshbandiyya, Chishtiyya, and Suhrawardiyya.

Wahhabism/Salafism

A strict, puritanical interpretation of Sunni Islam that emerged in the 18th century in the Arabian Peninsula, founded by Muhammad ibn Abd al-Wahhab. Wahhabism seeks to return Islam to what its proponents consider the "pure" practices of the early Muslims, rejecting innovations (bid'ah) and any form of intercession (such as visiting saints' graves). It is the dominant form of Islam in Saudi Arabia.

Ahmadiyya

Founded in the late 19th century by Mirza Ghulam Ahmad in India, the Ahmadiyya community believes in the idea of a reformist Messiah. Ahmadis consider Mirza Ghulam Ahmad as the promised Messiah and Mahdi, which distinguishes them from both Sunni and Shia Islam. This belief has led to significant opposition from mainstream Muslim groups, especially in countries like Pakistan where Ahmadis face legal persecution.

Ibadi Islam

The Ibadi sect is a branch of Islam that originated in the early period of Islam, during the time of the Khawarij. Ibadi Muslims are distinct from both Sunni and Shia Islam, though they share some characteristics with both. They are primarily found in Oman, and their views on governance and leadership differ from the mainstream Sunni and Shia traditions.

Kharijites

One of the earliest sects to emerge in Islam, the Kharijites were a faction that broke away from Ali's camp during the first Fitna (656–661 CE). They were known for their extreme views on takfir (declaring other Muslims as unbelievers) and their rejection of leadership based on lineage. While the Kharijites were largely wiped out, their ideology influenced later radical groups.

Ahl al-Hadith

A movement within Sunni Islam that emphasizes strict adherence to the Hadiths (sayings and actions of Prophet Muhammad) over any form of personal interpretation or the use of reason in deriving Islamic law. While not a separate sect, the Ahl al-Hadith movement has a significant following, especially in South Asia.

> *"And hold firmly together to the rope of Allah and do not be divided. Remember Allah's favour upon you when you were enemies, then He united your hearts, so you—by His grace—became brothers. And you were at the brink of a fiery pit and He saved you from it. This is how Allah makes His revelations clear to you, so that you may be rightly guided. (Quran 3:103)"*

Step-3

Can't break by Divisions?

Spread DISBELIEF!

The modern schooling system, as it exists today across the world, is not designed to nurture independent thinkers or individuals who question the deeper aspects of life, including spirituality, purpose, and morality. Instead, it subtly distances children from their faith, instills materialistic values, and molds them into obedient workers who serve the interests of a corporate-driven society rather than fulfilling their true potential.

Elon Musk, dissatisfied with traditional education systems, established Ad Astra in 2014, a private school designed to provide a unique learning environment for his children and the offspring of SpaceX employees. The school's name, meaning "To the stars" in Latin, reflects its forward-thinking approach. He has shared insights into his educational philosophy and the motivations behind creating his own school. Here are some notable quotes from him...

"I just didn't see that regular schools were doing the things I thought should be done. I thought, let's see what we can do. Maybe creating a school would be better."

"There aren't any grades... making all the children go in the same grade at the same time like an assembly line, because some people love English or languages. Some people love math. Some people love music. Different abilities, different times. It makes more sense to cater the education to match their aptitudes and abilities."

"It's important to teach problem solving, or teach to the problem and not the tools. Let's say you're trying to teach people about how engines work. A more traditional approach would be to say, 'we're going to teach all about screwdrivers and wrenches'... and you're going to have a course on screwdrivers and a course on wrenches. This is a very difficult way to do it. A much better way would be like, 'here's the engine. Now let's take it apart. How are we going to take it apart? Ah! You need a screwdriver. That's what the screwdriver is for. You need a wrench, that's what the wrench is for.' And then a very important thing happens: The relevance of the tools becomes apparent."

Now, the schooling system that is followed throughout the world today was designed and funded by John D. Rockefeller, a leading American industrialist who needed devoted workers for his industries, men who only know that he wants them to know and do what they are told without any doubts or questions. Quoting this man...

"I believe it is a religious duty to get all the money you can, fairly and honestly; to keep all you can, and to give away all you can"

TIME Magazine (21. May 1928)

"I would rather hire a man with enthusiasm, than a man who knows everything."

Classic Wisdom for the Professional Life (2010)

"I don't want a nation of thinkers, I want a nation of workers"

Jim Marrs in the William Lewis film One Nation Under Siege (2008)

Let's compare the Musk Model to the Rockefeller or Our Education model.

Purpose & Philosophy

Musk

Focuses on individualized learning rather than a one-size-fits-all curriculum. Encourages problem-solving over rote memorization. Emphasizes critical thinking and real-world applications. Allows students to progress at their own pace, catering to their natural talents and interests.

Rockefeller

Designed to produce workers and employees, not thinkers or innovators. Promotes a standardized curriculum, treating education like an assembly line. Emphasizes obedience, routine, and conformity over creativity. Discourages critical thinking and trains students to follow instructions rather than question systems.

Learning Style & Content

Musk

No grades or age-based segregation—students learn at their own pace. Subjects are taught through real-world problem-solving instead of isolated topics. Focus on STEM (Science, Technology, Engineering, Mathematics) with a hands-on, experimental approach. Prioritizes interdisciplinary learning, where subjects are combined (e.g., learning physics through building robots).

Rockefeller

Uses grades and rigid age divisions, forcing students into a standardized progression. Focuses on textbook-based learning, often detached from practical applications. Promotes subjects segregated into isolated fields, limiting interdisciplinary understanding. Instills a "memorize and reproduce" mentality rather than hands-on problem-solving.

Impact on Students

Musk

Produces critical thinkers, innovators, and leaders who challenge norms. Encourages entrepreneurial mindsets, self-learning, and adaptability. Helps students understand the world through experimentation rather than authority-imposed facts.

Rockefeller

Produces obedient workers who follow commands without questioning. Prepares students for 9-to-5 jobs rather than innovation or leadership roles. Promotes dependency on authority, discouraging students from questioning the system.

Psychological & Social Conditioning

Musk

Encourages independence and self-discovery. Instills confidence in challenging established ideas. Gives students the freedom to explore different career paths based on their passion.

Rockefeller

Trains children to be submissive to corporate structures and government authority. Instills a fear of failure through excessive grading and exams. Encourages materialism and financial dependence, making students value jobs over self-reliance.

Economic & Political Agenda

Musk

Aims to develop future innovators and pioneers in technology and science. Encourages entrepreneurship and self-sufficiency. Challenges traditional schooling norms, which could disrupt corporate control over education.

Rockefeller

Created to produce industrial workers who would serve corporations and maintain the capitalist system. Discourages self-employment or questioning of authority. Designed to suppress revolutionary thought, keeping power in the hands of elites.

Analysis

Undermining Faith Through Scientific Narratives

From the very beginning, children are taught a worldview that removes Allah from the equation. Science textbooks, rather than acknowledging the existence of a Creator, present nature as a self-sustaining, self-developing entity. The Big Bang theory is framed as a purely accidental event, evolution is taught as an autonomous process without divine intervention, and the universe is portrayed as something that formed itself through random occurrences.

This consistent narrative has a profound effect on young minds. When children are repeatedly told that everything is a product of chance, they begin to question the necessity of a Creator. Over time, this breeds atheistic or agnostic thinking at a large scale, leading to a society that sees religion as unnecessary or outdated. Even among those who maintain religious beliefs, many subconsciously separate faith from science, thinking that the two cannot coexist.

Suppressing Critical Thinking & Intellectual Curiosity

The current education system focuses almost entirely on rote memorization rather than deep understanding. Students are trained to follow instructions, memorize facts, and regurgitate information for exams, rather than developing critical thinking skills. This creates a generation of individuals who do not question the narratives they are fed, whether political, economic, or social.

More importantly, schools provide no real education on essential life skills. How to manage finances, pay taxes, understand governance, think critically, solve real-world problems, or become a better human being—none of these are prioritized. Instead, students are confined to classrooms where they passively absorb pre-approved information without questioning its validity.

The Rockefeller Influence: Creating Workers, Not Leaders

This system of education is not accidental; it was deliberately designed to create workers, not thinkers. The

Rockefeller Foundation, one of the key financial backers of modern schooling systems, openly admitted that they did not want a society of independent, self-sufficient individuals. Instead, their aim was to produce obedient workers who would sustain corporate industries. Schools train children to wake up early, follow strict schedules, obey rules, and work under authority—all preparing them to become employees who fit seamlessly into the corporate machine. The concept of the 9-to-5 job is instilled from a young age, teaching people that their only purpose in life is to work, earn, and consume.

Materialism: The Ultimate Trap

From childhood, people are conditioned to believe that success is measured only by money, degrees, and job titles. Parents, influenced by the same system, push their children toward careers that offer high salaries rather than personal fulfillment or religious growth. The narrative is simple:

Study hard → Get good grades → Get a degree → Secure a high-paying job → Earn more money → Buy expensive things → Repeat.

This cycle ensures that people remain enslaved to the economic system. They work overtime to afford a lifestyle dictated by consumerism. They are encouraged to buy more, spend more, and remain in constant debt, which keeps them dependent on the same corporate elites who control the system.

Psychological Conditioning: Destroying Self-Worth & Independence

One of the most subtle but powerful forms of psychological conditioning in schools is teaching students to ask for permission for everything—even drinking water. This might seem like a minor rule, but in reality, it subconsciously trains individuals to seek approval before fulfilling even their basic needs. As adults, these same individuals enter the workforce where they instinctively follow orders without questioning. They do not challenge their employers, do not fight for their rights, and do not aspire to become leaders. Instead, they remain passive, obedient workers, just as the system intended.

The Ultimate Goal: A Society Without Independent Thinkers

The schooling system does not create leaders, reformers, or visionaries—it creates followers. Those who dare to think beyond the system, those who seek knowledge beyond textbooks, and those who refuse to conform are often labeled as troublemakers, radicals, or outcasts.

A society that lacks critical thinkers and spiritual awareness is easier to control. When people are too busy working, paying off debts, and chasing material success, they have no time to reflect on their true purpose in life. They do not question political oppression, economic injustice, or moral decay—they simply exist to serve the system.

Step-4

Can't spread Disbelief?

DISTRACT!

In today's world, media and entertainment have become powerful tools for shaping minds, influencing beliefs, and controlling societies. From news channels and social media to music, movies, and the porn industry, every platform is designed to distract, manipulate, and weaken moral values—especially targeting the Muslim Ummah. Without realizing it, people are fed false narratives, addicted to mindless content, and distanced from their faith.

> *"This worldly life is no more than play and amusement, but far better is the eternal Home of the Hereafter for those mindful of Allah. Will you not then understand? (Quran 6:32)"*

> *"Know that this worldly life is no more than play, amusement, luxury, mutual boasting, and competition in wealth and children. This is like rain that causes plants to grow, to the delight of the planters. But later the plants dry up and you see them wither, then they are reduced to chaff. And in the Hereafter there will be either severe punishment or forgiveness and pleasure of Allah, whereas the life of this world is no more than the delusion of*

enjoyment. (Quran 57:20)"

News

Mainstream news channels are not independent sources of information—they are propaganda machines designed to push specific narratives that benefit global elites. Almost all major news networks are owned by the same industries and corporations, ensuring that they all deliver a coordinated message. Almost every major news network—CNN, BBC, Fox News, MSNBC etc are owned by a few powerful corporations that serve the interests of Western governments and industries. They do not report news; they manufacture public opinion.

Promoting Islamophobia

Media has continuously framed Muslims as terrorists, backward, or oppressive. Any crime committed by a Muslim is linked to Islam, while crimes by non-Muslims are attributed to "mental health issues" or isolated incidents.

Lying About Global Conflicts

News channels selectively show or suppress information to serve political goals. Wars in Palestine, Iraq, Syria, and Afghanistan have been covered from a biased perspective, justifying Western aggression while demonizing resistance movements.

Controlling Political Thought

Governments work hand in hand with media houses to shape public opinion. During elections, protests, or wars, the media manufactures consent so that people unknowingly support oppressive policies.

24/7 Fear and Distraction

News channels constantly bombard people with fear-mongering and distractions, whether it's economic crashes, pandemics, or celebrity scandals, so that the masses remain anxious, confused, and easily manipulated.

Jew founded news broadcasts, asset management and world banking affairs -

- Reuven Frank - NBC news
- Sandy Grushow - Fox news
- Larry Fink - Blackrock
- stephen Schwartzman - Blackstone
- Rothschild - Rothschild and Co
- Ben Bernanke - Federal Reserve

Youtube

The modern generation of children is not being raised by parents—it is being raised by YouTube and digital screens. Platforms like YouTube have become digital "babysitters," and the biggest channels targeting children use psychological manipulation to keep kids addicted.

Use of High-Saturation Colors and Fast-Paced Imagery

Popular children's shows like Cocomelon, Baby Shark, and others use bright, high-saturation colors and ultra-fast scene changes to overstimulate a child's brain. This leads to addiction and damages attention span development.

Repetitive Sounds and Patterns

Many kids' videos use repetitive songs and speech patterns that act like hypnotic triggers, keeping children glued to screens for hours. This early exposure to screen addiction damages natural brain development.

Delayed Speech and Cognitive Decline

Studies show that children who consume too much digital content have delayed speech development, weaker social skills, and poor cognitive abilities compared to those who engage in real-world activities.

Over-Dependence on Screens

Instead of playing outside, reading books, or developing skills, children today are hooked to tablets and smartphones, making them mentally weaker, emotionally fragile, and socially isolated.

Subliminal Messaging in Content

Many children's shows subtly introduce gender confusion, LGBTQ+ themes, and rebellion against parents, normalizing unnatural behaviors at an early age. The result is a generation of children who struggle to think critically, lack patience, and become passive consumers—exactly what the global elites want.

Social Media

Social media is the most addictive tool ever created to control minds. People today cannot live without scrolling through Instagram, TikTok, or Twitter. The goal is to keep people so distracted that they never stop to think about their real purpose in life.

Designed for Addiction

Platforms like TikTok and Instagram use AI to track your behavior and feed you content that keeps you scrolling for hours. This addiction destroys productivity, focus, and mental well-being.

Normalizing Immorality

Social media glorifies materialism, sexual content, and useless trends, corrupting minds—especially of the youth. What was once considered shameless is now promoted as "empowerment" or "self-expression."

Weakening the Muslim Ummah

Instead of reading the Quran or discussing important issues, the Muslim youth today are obsessed with influencers, celebrity gossip, and viral trends, leading to a weaker and less aware Ummah.

AI Control Over Thought

Social media decides what people see and believe. Political opinions, religious debates, and even personal ideologies are shaped by what the algorithm allows. Anything against the mainstream narrative is silenced or shadow-banned.

A small list of Jews involved-

- Larry ellison - Oracle
- Larry Page - Google /Alphabet
- Steve Ballmer - Microsoft
- Michael Bloomberg- Bloomberg
- Michael Dell - Dell
- Mark Zuckerberg - Meta
- Jan koum - Whatsapp
- Terry Semel- Yahoo
- Jeff Bezos - Amazon

Music

> *"Narrated Abu 'Amir or Abu Malik Al-Ash'ari that he heard the Prophet(peace be upon him) saying, "From among my followers there will be some people who will consider illegal sexual intercourse, the wearing of silk, the drinking of alcoholic drinks and the use of musical instruments, as lawful. (Sahih Al Bukhari 5590)"*

The music industry has become an open worship of Satanic ideologies. Many top artists openly use Satanic symbols, perform rituals on stage, and promote drug abuse, lust, and rebellion.

Satanic Symbolism in Music

Over the past decade, more and more artists are incorporating Satanic imagery into their music videos and performances. Artists like Lil Nas X, Beyoncé, and Rihanna have been caught in high-profile performances where they openly mock religious themes, glorify Satan, or engage in occult rituals. These performances are not mere coincidences; they are intentional acts designed to push the boundaries of morality and normalize rebellion against divine law.

Normalization of Immorality

Music videos frequently glorify drug use, promiscuity, and violence. Lyrics often promote destructive lifestyles, and the "bad boy/girl" image is constantly idealized. Through catchy tunes and seductive imagery, the music industry pushes messages that encourage individuals—especially impressionable youth—to reject moral principles in favor of instant gratification and self-destructive behavior. This reinforces the values of consumerism and hedonism, diverting focus away from spiritual growth.

> *"It was narrated from Abu Malik Ash'ari that the Messenger of Allah (peace be upon him) said: "People among my nation will drink wine, calling it by another name, and musical instruments will be played for them and singing girls (will sing for them). Allah will cause the earth to swallow them up, and will turn them into monkeys and pigs." (Sahih ibn Majah 4020)"*

Quran cannot enter a heart in which music is present

The Quran advises Muslims to protect their hearts from distractions and sinful influences, as the heart is the primary vessel for guidance and faith. In this context, music, particularly the type that contains negative or distracting messages, can hinder the ability of the heart to receive the divine words of Allah. Islamic scholars often highlight that listening to music, especially if it contains inappropriate themes or is performed in ways that lead to indulgence in worldly desires, can dull a person's spiritual sensitivity. It is believed that when a person exposes themselves to harmful entertainment, it creates a barrier between them and their ability to focus on the sacred and pure teachings of the Quran. The Quran calls for mindfulness, reflection, and sincerity when approaching Allah's word, and distractions like music, which often evoke emotions that lead away from spiritual contemplation, can create obstacles to that deeper connection.

> "*Narrated Abdullah ibn Umar: Nafi' said: Ibn Umar heard a pipe, put his fingers in his ears and went away from the road. He said to me: Are you hearing anything? I said: No. He said: He then took his fingers out of his ears and said: I was with the Prophet(peace be upon him), and he heard like this and he did like this. AbuAli al-Lu'lu said: I heard AbuDawud say: This is a rejected tradition. (Sunan abi Dawood 4924)*"

List of Jews involved-

- Herb Abramson- Atlantic Records
- Berle Adams - Mercury Records
- Marty Bandier- Sony
- Jerry Blaine - Jubilee Records
- Allen Klein - The Rolling Stones

Movies

The movie industry is one of the most powerful tools used by global elites to shape culture, manipulate public opinion, and promote ideologies that often go against moral and religious principles. Movies have the ability to influence millions of people worldwide, making them an ideal medium for pushing narratives that promote materialism, secularism, and even immoral behavior. Over the years, the movie industry has been used not only to entertain but also to serve a broader agenda aimed at controlling the masses.

Glorification of Immorality

Movies often glamorize immoral behavior like violence, crime, and promiscuity. Criminals are presented as heroes in films, making illegal actions appear desirable. Similarly, casual sex is normalized in romantic comedies and dramas, weakening traditional family values and promoting a disregard for commitment.

Promotion of Secularism and Materialism

Movies promote a materialistic worldview where success is measured by wealth and power. Films prioritize money and fame as markers of achievement, ignoring deeper values like community and spirituality. Many films also portray secular narratives, suggesting that life can be lived without reference to religion or higher purpose.

Political Agenda and Social Engineering

Movies often carry political messages that reflect the agenda of the elites controlling the media. Films subtly shape opinions on social issues like race, gender, and politics, reinforcing liberal ideologies and normalizing changes like LGBTQ+ acceptance, which influences societal beliefs and behaviors.

Creating Dependence on Entertainment

Movies distract from meaningful activities by providing an emotional escape. As people become dependent on entertainment, they lose agency and miss opportunities for personal and intellectual growth. This dependence fosters passivity, making individuals less likely to reflect on their purpose or engage in self-improvement.

A small list of Jews involved-

- Avi Arad- Marvel
- Ted Ashley- Warner Bros
- Barney Balaban- Paramount Pictures
- Gary Barber- Metro Goldwyn Mayer, Spyglass
- Alan Braverman- Walt Disney company
- Harry Cohn- Columbia pictures
- William goetz - 20h Century Fox
- Marc Randolph- Netflix

Pornography

"O Prophet! Tell the believing men to lower their gaze and guard their chastity. That is purer for them. Surely Allah is All-Aware of what they do. (Quran 24:30)"

"Do not go near adultery. It is truly a shameful deed and an evil way. (Quran 17:32)"

The pornography industry is one of the most destructive forces in modern society. It is a multi-billion-dollar industry that thrives on exploiting human vulnerabilities, addiction, and objectification of individuals, especially women. While the industry is largely controlled by a small group of Jewish entrepreneurs, its harmful impact on society extends far beyond its profit margins.

Destruction of Relationships

Porn addiction has been shown to lead to impaired relationships, as individuals become more fixated on virtual experiences than on cultivating real, meaningful relationships. This addiction leads to feelings of guilt, shame, and emotional numbness, and it creates an environment where love and respect are replaced by lust and objectification.

Normalization of Objectification

Pornography objectifies women, reducing them to mere commodities used for male pleasure. This contributes to gender inequality, sexism, and the growing culture of rape. Women are exploited, trafficked, and often coerced into the industry, with little regard for their mental and emotional well-being.

Addiction and Control

Studies have shown that frequent consumption of pornography rewires the brain, creating a dopamine addiction similar to other forms of substance abuse. Those who are addicted to porn are more likely to desensitize themselves to normal sexual encounters, leading to the need for ever more extreme content. This ensures that individuals remain trapped in a cycle of addiction, unable to break free from the grip of materialism and lust.

> *"Marry off the free singles among you, as well as the righteous of your bondmen and bondwomen. If they are poor, Allah will enrich them out of His bounty. For Allah is All-Bountiful, All-Knowing. (Quran 24:32)"*

- Alvin goldstein
- Solomon Friedman
- Reuben Starman
- Bernd Bergmair
- Fabian Thylmann

CHAPTER IV

Aghaaz-e-Ikhtitaam

The modern world is filled with distractions designed to keep people occupied with unnecessary activities, leaving them no time to reflect on their faith or the deeper realities of life. Movies, music, pornography, social media, and the endless cycle of consumerism have created a society that is lost in entertainment and materialism. The result is a generation disconnected from Islam, unaware of the prophetic warnings about the future, and completely blind to the forces shaping the world toward the coming of Dajjal.

This is not an accident; it is a deliberate system created by Western leaders and influential elites, many of whom work together to establish a new world order—one global government, one rule, and ultimately, a system designed to pave the way for the appearance of Dajjal. By keeping the Ummah distracted, addicted, and intellectually weakened, they ensure that when Dajjal claims to be God and performs his deceptive "miracles," many Muslims, disconnected from Allah, will follow him blindly.

These distractions are not just random elements of entertainment; they are part of a larger strategy to keep the world busy while the elites reshape global power. The new world order is not just a theory—it is an openly stated goal of powerful organizations that seek to unite the world under one government, one financial system, and ultimately, one ruler.

Why would a Muslim who does not care about his own parents, care about the Ummah?

A generation that sees material possessions as the purpose of life, where buying an iPhone or a luxury car has become the purpose of life rather than seeking knowledge or standing against oppression.

When the new world order is fully in place, when laws are passed that strip people of their freedoms, when Dajjal finally emerges claiming to be God and showing his deceptive "miracles," this lost generation will not be able to resist. They will have spent their entire lives immersed in entertainment, their hearts disconnected from Allah, their minds too weak to recognize the deception. They will follow him blindly, believing in his false promises, because they never took the time to understand the truth of their own religion.

This is not just a warning—it is a call to action. The enemies of Islam are not waiting. They are using every possible method, every technological advancement, and every psychological trick to ensure that their agenda succeeds. If Muslims do not wake up now, if they do not return to their deen, strengthen their faith, and reject these distractions, they will find themselves too late to act when the final deception unfolds.

THE ILLUMINATI

The Illuminati is described as a secret society working behind the scenes to control governments, economies, and societal trends. Founded in 1776 by Adam Weishaupt in Bavaria (modern-day Germany), the Illuminati is a secret society dedicated to enlightenment principles, such as reason, freedom of thought, and opposition to religious and political oppression. The group sought to infiltrate influential institutions like governments, universities, and churches to spread their ideals.

Global Domination

Establishing a New World Order (NWO) where a single authoritarian government controls the planet.

Control Over Population

Through surveillance, propaganda, and economic manipulation, the Illuminati allegedly seeks to enslave humanity.

Erasure of Religion

The group is often accused of promoting atheism or satanism, aiming to undermine traditional religious beliefs.

Cultural Engineering

Shaping public values and attitudes through control of the media, entertainment, and education systems.

Influence Over Global Institutions

The Illuminati is alleged to control major organizations like the United Nations, the World Bank, the International Monetary Fund (IMF), and even tech giants like Google and Microsoft. It is also accused of manipulating the global financial system through central banks, particularly the Federal Reserve and BIS (Bank for International Settlements).

Recruitment of Global Elites

Prominent figures in politics, business, entertainment, and academia are rumored to be Illuminati members. These include U.S. presidents, Hollywood celebrities, and CEOs of multinational corporations. Events like the Bilderberg Group meetings and Bohemian Grove gatherings are often cited as forums for Illuminati planning.

Media and Entertainment Control

Uses Hollywood, music, and mainstream media to manipulate public opinion. Celebrities like Beyoncé, Jay-Z, Kanye West, and Rihanna are frequently accused of being members or puppets of the Illuminati. Subliminal messages in music videos, movies, and advertisements are cited as tools to normalize the Illuminati's agenda.

Staged Global Events

Natural disasters, terrorist attacks, and pandemics are sometimes labeled as orchestrated by the Illuminati to maintain control or distract the population. Events like 9/11, the COVID-19 pandemic, and financial crashes are linked to their long-term plans.

Depopulation Agenda

The Illuminati is often accused of promoting depopulation through vaccines, GMOs, wars, and economic policies. This ties into fears of a one-world government controlling every aspect of life.

New World Order (NWO)

The ultimate goal of the Illuminati is to establish a New World Order—a unified global government where freedoms are suppressed, and power rests in the hands of a few elites.

PROJECT BLUE BEAM

Project Blue Beam is a popular theory that suggests a global effort to create a New World Order (NWO) by using advanced technology to simulate a fake alien invasion or religious events. The theory was popularized by Serge Monast, a Canadian journalist, in the 1990s. He claimed that governments, in collaboration with powerful organizations like NASA and the United Nations, would use this project to manipulate and control humanity, and their main aim is to abolish all religions and create a single, atheistic global religion, to establish a one-world government controlled by an elite group and to enforce control over humanity through fear and manipulation.

A Fake Universal Religion

According to Monast, the project would aim to replace existing religions with one universal religion. This would involve the use of holographic projections of religious figures (like Prophets, Angels, or Buddha) appearing in the skies worldwide, tailored to specific regions.

Simulated Alien Invasion

Advanced holographic and sound technology would be used to simulate an alien invasion, creating fear and panic to push humanity into accepting a unified global government.

Mind Control via Technology

The theory suggests that electromagnetic and psychological warfare would be employed to manipulate people's thoughts, making them more compliant with the New World Order.

Global Crisis Creation

Natural disasters, wars, and economic collapses would be orchestrated to destabilize nations and pave the way for a single governing authority.

Use of HAARP and Satellites

Monast linked Project Blue Beam to technologies like HAARP (High-Frequency Active Auroral Research Program), which he claimed could manipulate weather and cause natural disasters.

AGENDA 21/30

Despite its non-binding nature, Agenda 21 has become a central element in various conspiracy theories. Critics claim that it is part of a globalist plot aimed at creating a New World Order (NWO) and eroding national sovereignty.

Centralized Control of Land and Resources

Agenda 21 calls for the centralized control of land and natural resources, leading to a loss of private property rights. It promotes "land use planning" that limits the amount of land available for individuals, forcing people into tightly controlled urban environments. Critics argue that this could lead to "smart cities", where every aspect of life—housing, travel, energy use—is monitored and controlled by the state.

Population Control

Agenda 21 seeks to reduce the global population through fertility control, forced sterilization, and other means. The argument is that with the world's growing population, sustainable development will require reducing the number of people, often referring to the so-called "population control" element within the agenda.

Loss of Sovereignty

Critics claim that Agenda 21 undermines national sovereignty by promoting international governance.

Governments may cede power to global organizations like the United Nations, leaving local governments with reduced authority. The theory suggests that international bodies would impose top-down regulations that dictate everything from urban zoning to individual consumption.

Reduction of Personal Freedoms

It will lead to increased surveillance and control, forcing people to give up their freedoms in the name of "sustainability." Critics argue that efforts to reduce carbon footprints, limit car ownership, and push for public transportation systems could restrict people's ability to travel freely and independently.

Environmentalism as a Cover for Authoritarianism

The theory claims that the emphasis on environmental protection is a smokescreen for implementing a totalitarian regime where individual rights are subjugated to a global agenda. Governments may use climate change and sustainability issues as justification to increase control over people's daily lives and implement restrictive policies under the guise of environmentalism.

THE GREAT RESET

The Great Reset is a concept introduced by the World Economic Forum (WEF) in June 2020, primarily driven by its founder Klaus Schwab. The official intention of the Great Reset is to address the social, economic, and environmental impacts of the pandemic and build a more resilient, sustainable world, theorists argue that it represents a deliberate attempt by the global elite to reshape the world in their favor, centralize power, and strip individuals of their freedoms.

Centralization of Power and Control

One of the central claims of the Great Reset conspiracy is that global elites, particularly through organizations like the WEF, are using the pandemic as a catalyst to centralize power and control the world's economies and political systems.

Global Governance

The theory suggests that global organizations, such as the United Nations, the World Health Organization (WHO), and the International Monetary Fund (IMF), are being used to undermine national sovereignty and force nations into a global governance system where individual countries lose autonomy.

Technocratic Control

It is suggested that the elite would use technocracy (rule by technical experts) to impose a new world order, where economic, political, and social decisions are made by an unelected, technocratic elite, often using technology as the backbone for surveillance and social control.

Economic Reformation and Wealth Redistribution

Another major aspect of the Great Reset theory is the belief that the WEF's economic vision is designed to redistribute wealth, though not necessarily in a way that benefits the broader global population. Critics argue that the reset could accelerate the wealth gap by shifting resources from ordinary people to corporate interests and global elites.

Universal Basic Income (UBI)

UBI (a concept discussed as part of the Great Reset) would be implemented as a means of controlling populations, ensuring that citizens are dependent on government handouts, rather than having the freedom or means to resist control.

Wealth Redistribution

While proponents of the Great Reset argue for fairer wealth distribution to address inequality, critics fear that this could lead to a centralized redistribution of resources controlled by powerful institutions, rather than solving systemic issues of poverty and inequality.

Surveillance and Social Credit Systems

A pervasive aspect of the Great Reset conspiracy is the claim that it will usher in a surveillance state designed to track and monitor individual behavior. This is tied to the increasing use of digital currencies, biometric identification, and digital passports that would allow authorities to track every aspect of a person's life.

Global Resource Control

The theory suggests that a handful of powerful entities could control natural resources, such as water, food, and energy, in ways that would make people reliant on centralized systems. Resource scarcity, driven by artificial policies or engineered crises, is often viewed as a strategy to enforce population control.

Microchip Implants and Digital Currencies

The topics of microchip implants and digital currencies have become central to various theories about a New World Order (NWO), global control, and the erosion of privacy and freedom.

Global Tracking and Surveillance

A prevalent theory posits that microchips could be used to track every individual's movements and activities in real-time. This would provide governments or powerful organizations with the ability to monitor and control every aspect of people's lives, from their location to their personal habits, without consent. Proponents of this theory argue that mass implantation of microchips would make it nearly impossible for people to hide their actions, thus eliminating privacy and autonomy.

Totalitarian Control

Many conspiracy theorists claim that the widespread use of microchips would create a totalitarian society, where governments or global organizations could use the chips to control individuals. This could include tracking behaviors, restricting movements, or even controlling who can participate in social or economic systems. There is a fear that microchips could be used as a tool for compliance, where people might be denied access to food, healthcare, or employment if they are not implanted or are seen as "undesirable."

Loss of Free Will and Autonomy

The microchips could interfere with people's free will by altering thoughts, behaviors, or even memories. They believe that as these technologies advance, chips could be used not just for tracking, but for controlling human thoughts or decisions, pushing individuals into conformity with the desires of those in power.

Compulsory Chip Implantation

Another fear is that microchip implantation might one day become mandatory for everyone, especially with the advent of "digital ID" systems or "cashless societies". The belief is that governments or corporations might require all citizens to receive an implant for identification, security, or access to services, leading to the loss of freedom.

Centralized Bank Digital Currency (CBDC) as a Tool for Total Control

Governments are increasingly exploring the idea of Central Bank Digital Currencies (CBDCs), which would be state-controlled, digital versions of fiat currencies (like the US dollar or the euro). This will lead to a cashless society, where people would have no access to physical currency and all transactions would be conducted digitally. This would allow governments to monitor every transaction, control how and when people can spend their money, and implement policies such as negative interest rates (where money can expire or lose value over time).

Elimination of Privacy

With all transactions tracked digitally, individuals would lose the ability to make anonymous transactions, leading to fears of total financial surveillance. People would no longer be able to purchase goods or services without the government or central authority knowing about it. This could also extend to social credit systems, where people's spending behavior, savings, and investments could be used to evaluate their "social score" or loyalty to the system, potentially impacting their access to certain goods, services, or even travel.

Cryptocurrencies as a Tool for Elite Control

While many see cryptocurrencies like Bitcoin as a way to avoid government control, theorists argue that global elites could manipulate the market for personal gain. They argue that wealthy individuals or corporations could use cryptocurrencies to destabilize economies, furthering their control over the masses.

PHARMACEUTICS

The term "Big Pharma" refers to the powerful multinational pharmaceutical companies that dominate the global healthcare industry. These companies prioritize profits over patient welfare, manipulate medical research, suppress cures, and influence global health policies to maintain their power. These theories claim that the pharmaceutical industry is engaged in a coordinated effort to control global health, monopolize drug markets, and suppress alternative treatments that could threaten their profits.

Suppression of Cures and Natural Remedies

Big Pharma deliberately suppresses natural cures or alternative treatments to diseases in favor of expensive pharmaceutical drugs. Theorists argue that natural remedies or non-patented treatments for serious conditions such as cancer, diabetes, and HIV/AIDS are intentionally buried to maintain pharmaceutical profits.

Cancer Cures

The natural cures for cancer—including herbal remedies, vitamin therapies, and alternative medicines—are deliberately ignored or repressed by the pharmaceutical industry. Some theorists argue that these treatments would be far more effective, but that companies stand to lose billions in revenue if these alternatives were to gain popularity.

Drugs like Ivermectin and Fenbendazole have been found effective in treating even stage 4 cancer, yet they remain unheard of.

Suppressed Technologies

Another facet involves claims that certain innovative medical technologies or cures are intentionally hidden from the public because they don't align with the industry's business models. The example often cited is the suppression of cancer treatment technologies such as high-dose vitamin C, or treatments based on cannabis, baking soda, and other natural substances.

Pharmaceutical Lobbying and Political Influence

Big Pharma has an immense lobbying power, enabling them to shape public policy and laws that are favorable to the pharmaceutical industry at the expense of public health. They point to large sums of money spent on political donations, lobbying, and research funding as evidence of corporate influence.

Regulatory Capture

The theory claims that government agencies like the U.S. Food and Drug Administration (FDA) or European Medicines Agency (EMA) are influenced or controlled by pharmaceutical companies. This is known as regulatory capture, where the interests of private companies overshadow the public interest, resulting in weak regulations, loopholes, and uncritical approval of new drugs.

Price Gouging

High-profile cases of drug price gouging have contributed to the theory, such as when Martin Shkreli, the CEO of Turing Pharmaceuticals and Vyera Pharmaceuticals, dramatically raised the price of Daraprim, a drug used to treat toxoplasmosis in HIV/AIDS patients, by more than 5,000%(around 740$ per pill). Such incidents fuel the belief that the pharmaceutical industry is intentionally exploiting vulnerable patients for profit.

Inaccessibility of Life-saving Medications

The rising cost of essential medications, such as insulin, has sparked outrage and further strengthened the idea that pharmaceutical companies are deliberately pricing out the majority of people from access to life-saving drugs.

Vaccine Safety Concerns

The pharmaceutical industry is intentionally downplaying or covering up the dangers associated with vaccines, such as side effects or long-term health impacts. This belief became particularly prominent during the debates surrounding the MMR vaccine (measles, mumps, rubella), which some claim is linked to autism, despite extensive research debunking this theory.

COVID-19 Vaccines

The COVID-19 pandemic and the subsequent vaccine rollout have intensified the theory that Big Pharma is using the pandemic as a means to profit from the mass production and global distribution of vaccines. The vaccines were rushed and unsafe, and the pharmaceutical companies are pushing for widespread adoption to maximize their profits.

Dr Ana Maria Mihalcea conducted a research on COVID-19 vaccine and during an interview on Child Health Defense, she said

"We did analysis of COVID-19 injection and found 54 undeclared chemical elements including fluorescent graphene oxide"

These are the chemicals responsible for diseases like Diabetes, Cancer, Heath Failure and others in vaccinated individuals.

HAARP and WEATHER CONTROL

The High-Frequency Active Auroral Research Program (HAARP) is a U.S.-based research initiative designed to study the ionosphere, a layer of Earth's atmosphere that plays a crucial role in radio wave propagation. Although officially intended for scientific purposes, HAARP has been at the center of numerous theories, which claim that it is a tool for weather manipulation, mind control, and military dominance.

Location: Gakona, Alaska.

Started: 1993, funded by the U.S. Air Force, Navy, and Defense Advanced Research Projects Agency (DARPA).

HAARP uses an array of high-frequency (HF) antennas to send focused electromagnetic waves into the ionosphere. This is intended to simulate natural disturbances, such as solar flares, to better understand their effects on satellite communication and military systems.

Weather Manipulation

Many theorists believe HAARP can create and control natural disasters, such as hurricanes, earthquakes, droughts, and floods.

The 2005 Hurricane Katrina disaster was blamed on HAARP by some theorists, who argued that the storm was "engineered" to target specific regions.

The 2010 Haiti Earthquake was also linked to HAARP, with claims that it was used to create seismic activity for political or economic gain.

Geophysical Warfare

The idea is that HAARP could be used as a weapon of mass destruction by targeting specific locations with weather disasters. Theorists cite documents like the U.S. military's "Weather as a Force Multiplier: Owning the Weather in 2025" to argue that weather control is part of a military strategy.

Mind Control

Some believe that HAARP's electromagnetic waves are designed to manipulate human behavior or emotions on a mass scale. This theory links HAARP to low-frequency waves (ELF waves), which, according to theorists, can interfere with human brain activity. Claims include inducing anxiety, depression, or apathy in populations to make them easier to control.

Climate Engineering and Chemtrails

HAARP is often tied to the chemtrail theory, which alleges that aircraft contrails contain chemicals sprayed to manipulate the climate or control populations. According to this theory, HAARP interacts with these chemicals to alter weather patterns or trigger health issues.

Evidence

Statements from Officials

The U.S. Air Force and DARPA's public admissions about studying the ionosphere for military purposes (e.g., communication with submarines) fuel suspicions about HAARP's potential to manipulate weather or act as a weapon.

Patent Documents

In the 1980s, Dr. Bernard Eastlund, a physicist, patented technology similar to HAARP's methodology, which theorists claim was capable of altering weather and even disrupting communication systems. This patent, along with Eastlund's statements, is often cited as "proof" that HAARP's technology has weaponized capabilities.

Unusual Weather Events

Theorists link HAARP to bizarre weather phenomena, such as unseasonal storms, unexplained heatwaves, or sudden temperature shifts. They argue that HAARP experiments leave detectable "signatures" in the atmosphere, visible as colorful auroras or strange cloud formations.

CHEMTRAILS

The "chemtrail" theory revolves around the belief that the white streaks left behind by aircraft, known as contrails (short for condensation trails), are not just water vapor but instead contain harmful chemicals intentionally sprayed into the atmosphere for secretive purposes. According to proponents of the theory, these "chemtrails" are part of covert government or corporate programs aimed at controlling the weather, population, or the environment.

Weather Modification (Geoengineering)

Chemtrails are part of geoengineering programs aimed at controlling the weather or combating climate change. One common claim is that these trails contain aluminum oxide, barium salts, and other reflective particles designed to block sunlight and reduce global warming. The supposed goal is to modify atmospheric conditions, such as inducing rain, dispersing storms, or artificially cooling the planet.

Population Control

Another claim is that chemtrails contain chemicals designed to control population growth by spreading infertility or diseases. Some theorists allege these chemicals are linked to a rise in respiratory illnesses, cancers, and neurological disorders.

Agricultural and Economic Gain

Chemtrails are accused of deliberately damaging crops and soils to benefit biotech companies, which develop genetically modified organisms (GMOs) that can withstand the chemical exposure.

Military Applications

Chemtrails are part of advanced military programs, such as creating weather-based weapons or disrupting enemy communication systems. Others link chemtrails to ionospheric research programs like HAARP, arguing the sprayed chemicals enhance electromagnetic experiments.

Substances found in Chemtrails

Aluminum Oxide

Claimed to be used for reflecting sunlight and altering weather patterns.

Barium Salts

Allegedly used to enhance electrical conductivity in the atmosphere, enabling weather manipulation or radar disruptions.

Strontium

Believed to affect health and fertility when inhaled over time.

Evidence

Chemical Analysis

Independent researchers have allegedly detected elevated levels of aluminum, barium, and other chemicals in soil and water samples in areas where chemtrails are visible.

Patents

Numerous patents exist for geoengineering technologies, including those involving aerosolized particles. These patents are often cited as proof that chemtrails are a reality. Patent US5003186, which outlines the use of stratospheric aerosol injections for altering the atmosphere.

Dr. Israr Ahmed extensively discussed the New World Order (NWO) and its deep connections with Zionist ambitions, Dajjal's arrival, and the end-times prophecies in Islam. He argued that the global elite, primarily influenced by Zionist agendas, are working systematically toward a global government that will eventually lead to the establishment of the throne of Dajjal. He outlined five key phases in this grand scheme...

ARMAGEDDON

In Islamic eschatology, it is referred to as the Battle of Armageddon or Malhama al-Kubra. In this scenario, a final confrontation takes place between the forces of Islam (led by the Mahdi) and the forces of evil (led by the Antichrist, or Dajjal). The Zionist-controlled Western powers are intentionally escalating global conflicts to lead the world into a final great war—Armageddon. A war between global superpowers (U.S., Russia, China, and Muslim nations) will break out. The Muslim world will suffer heavily, but some forces will stand against oppression. This will be a prelude to Dajjal's emergence and the final battles of truth vs. falsehood.

Prophet Muhammad(peace be upon him)spoke about a great war before the Day of Judgment, where Muslims will fight a powerful enemy near the region of Syria.

> *"Abu Huraira reported Allah's Messenger (peace be upon him) as saying: The Last Hour would not come until the Romans would land at al-A'maq or in Dabiq. An army consisting of the best (soldiers) of the people of the earth at that time will come from Medina (to counteract them). When they will*

arrange themselves in ranks, the Romans would say: Do not stand between us and those (Muslims) who took prisoners from amongst us. Let us fight with them; and the Muslims would say: Nay, by Allah, we would never get aside from you and from our brethren that you may fight them. They will then fight and a third (part) of the army would run away, whom Allah will never forgive. A third (part of the army) which would be constituted of excellent martyrs in Allah's eye, would be killed and the third who would never be put to trial would win and they would be conquerors of Constantinople. And as they would be busy in distributing the spoils of war (amongst themselves) after hanging their swords by the olive trees, the Satan would cry: The Dajjal has taken your place among your family. They would then come out, but it would be of no avail. And when they would come to Syria, he would come out while they would be still preparing themselves for battle drawing up the ranks. Certainly, the time of prayer shall come and then Jesus (peace be upon him) son of Mary would descend and would lead them. When the enemy of Allah would see him, it would (disappear) just as the salt dissolves itself in water and if he (Jesus) were not to confront them at all, even then it would dissolve completely, but Allah would kill them by his hand and he would show them their blood on his lance (the lance of Jesus Christ). (Sahih Muslim 2897)"

Dr. Israr linked this "Roman" force to Western military alliances like NATO, controlled by Zionists.

GREATER ISRAEL

The Zionist movement has a long-term objective of establishing "Greater Israel", which extends beyond present-day Israel into Palestine, Jordan, parts of Egypt, Syria, Iraq, and Saudi Arabia (including Makkah and Madinah). Destabilizing Muslim nations through war, political corruption, and economic collapse to remove any opposition because the Zionists believe that to bring their so-called Messiah (Dajjal), they must expand Israel and control the entire Middle East.

> *"And We conveyed to the Children of Israel in the Scripture that, 'You will surely cause corruption on the earth twice, and you will reach great heights of arrogance.(Quran 17:4)"*

According to Dr. Israr, the first corruption was their rejection of Prophets, and the second corruption is happening now through their global dominance and their control over media, banks, and world governments.

DEMOLITION OF AL-AQSA

One of the biggest goals of the Zionist elite is destroying Masjid Al-Aqsa to rebuild the Third Temple of Solomon. Continuous Israeli attacks on Masjid Al-Aqsa, archeological excavations under Al-Aqsa to weaken its structure, and settler expansions around Al-Aqsa to make it easier for demolition.

Prophet Muhammad(peace be upon him) warned that one of the greatest signs of the end times would be the destruction of Masjid Al-Aqsa.

"Narrated Mu'adh ibn Jabal: The Prophet(peace be upon him) said: The flourishing state of Jerusalem will be when Yathrib is in ruins, the ruined state of Yathrib will be when the great war comes, the outbreak of the great war will be at the conquest of Constantinople and the conquest of Constantinople when the Dajjal (Antichrist) comes forth. He (the Prophet) struck his thigh or his shoulder with his hand and said: This is as true as you are here or as you are sitting (meaning Mu'adh ibn Jabal). (Abu Dawood 4294)"

Once Al-Aqsa is destroyed, the Jewish elite will immediately start constructing the Third Temple, which will become the spiritual center of their global rule.

THE THIRD TEMPLE

Once the Zionists achieve their goal of demolishing Al-Aqsa, they plan to rebuild the Third Temple in its place. This temple will be the headquarters for the Antichrist (Dajjal), whom they mistakenly believe to be their Messiah. Zionist rabbis, Masonic lodges, and secret societies are all working toward this goal. The NWO is paving the way by controlling global politics, economies, and social systems.

The Prophet(peace be upon him) described that Dajjal will claim to be God, and his throne will be in Jerusalem.

"Anas b. Malik reported that Allah's Messenger (peace be upon him) said: There is never a prophet who has not warned the Ummah of that one-eyed liar; behold he is one-eyed and your Lord is not one-eyed. On his forehead are the letters k f. r. (Kafir).

(Sahih Muslim 2933)"

Dr. Israr Ahmed explained that Dajjal's rule is not just about military power—it is a global ideological war where people's minds are being prepared to accept him as a savior.

THE THRONE OF THE DEVIL

The New World Order is actually a Satanic plan designed to eliminate religious beliefs and moral values through media, education, and culture, creating a "one-world government" controlled by elites who worship the devil and control global wealth, food, and resources so that people are forced to obey them in order to prepare the world for the arrival of Dajjal.

Prophet Muhammad(peace be upon him) said that near the end times:

People will be deceived on a massive scale.

Wealth will be controlled by a few powerful hands.

Religious knowledge will disappear, and immorality will spread.

"*It was narrated from Abu Hurairah that the Messenger of Allah (peace be upon him) said: There will come to the people years of treachery, when the liar will be regarded as honest, and the honest man will be regarded as a liar; the traitor will be regarded as faithful, and the faithful man will be regarded as a traitor; and the Ruwaibidah will decide matters.' It was said: 'Who are the Ruwaibidah?' He said: 'Vile and base men who control the affairs of the people.' (Sunan Ibn Majah 4036)*"

CHAPTER V

Anjaam-e-Qaaynaat

QIYAMAH

Muslims today are so deeply absorbed in their personal lives, entertainment, and careers that they fail to see the world preparing against them. The signs of Qiyamah unfold before our eyes—widespread immorality, oppression, the destruction of values—yet we dismiss them as coincidences. Meanwhile, the enemies of Islam wage psychological and ideological warfare, conditioning minds and eroding faith to pave the way for Dajjal's deception. Despite having clear warnings in the Quran and Sunnah, many remain heedless. But when the sun rises from the west, sealing the doors of repentance, realization will come—too late.

THE MINOR SIGNS

Hadhrat Abu Musa Ash'ari radhiyallahu anhu narrates that the Prophet(peace be upon him) said , Qiyamah will come...

1.When it will be regarded as a shame to act on Quranic injunctions.

2.When untrustworthy people will be regarded as trustworthy and the trustworthy will be regarded as untrustworthy.

3.When it will be hot in winter (and vice versa).

4.When the length of days is stretched, i.e. a journey of a few days is covered in a matter of hours.

5.When orators and lecturers lie openly.

6.When people dispute over petty issues.

7.When women with children come displeased on account of them bearing offspring, and barren women remain happy on account of having no responsibility of offspring.

8.When oppression, jealousy, and greed become the order of the day.

9.When people blatantly follow their passions and whims.

10.When lies prevail over the truth.

11.When violence, bloodshed and anarchy become common.

12.When immorality overtakes shamelessness and is perpetrated publicly.

13.When legislation matters pertaining to Deen is handed over to the worst elements of the Ummat, and if people accept them and are satisfied with their findings, then such persons will not smell the fragrance of Jannat

14.When the offspring become a cause of grief and anger (for their parents).

The following is part of a lengthy Hadith narrated by Hadhrat Abdullah Ibn Mas'ood radhiyallahu anhu when he inquired from the Prophet (peace be upon him) about the Signs of Qiyamah.

1.Music and musical instruments will be found in every home.

2.People will indulge in homosexuality.

3.There will be an abundance of illegitimate children.

4.There will be an abundance of critics, tale-carriers, back- biters and taunters in society.

5.People will establish ties with strangers and sever relations with their near and dear ones.

6.Hypocrites will be in control of the affairs of the community and evil, immoral people will be at the helm of business establishments.

7.The Masjid will be decorated, but the hearts of the people will be devoid of guidance.

8.The courtyards of Masjids will be built beautifully and high mimbars (pulpits) will be erected.

9.Gangsters and evil people will prevail.

10.Various wines will be consumed excessively.

Auf bin Malik radhiyallahu anhu says: I came to the Prophet (peace be upon him) he was in his skin tent during the Tabuk expedition. He said to me, "Count six things before the advent of

Qiyamah:

1.My death

2.The conquest of Jerusalem

3.Mass deaths amongst you people, just as when sheep die in large numbers during an epidemic

4.Abundance of wealth to such an extent that if a person were to be given a hundred Dinars he will still not be satisfied

5.General anarchy and bloodshed, that no Arab household will be spared from it

6.Then a life of peace as a result of a peace agreement between you and the Banil Asfaar (Romans) which they will break and attack you with a force consisting of eighty flags and under each flag will be an army of twelve thousand men." (Hadith: Sahih Bukhari).

THE MAJOR SIGNS

The occurrences before the Major Signs:

GENOCIDE

A man from Abu Sufyaan's progeny massacres descendents of Nabi (S.A.W) and rules over Syria and Egypt.

WAR

A major war between Muslims and Christians: Half the Christian army will sign a peace treaty with the Muslim army, while the second half of the Christian army remains the common enemy.

ISTANBUL CONQUERED BY CHRISTIANS

The enemy half of the Christian army conquers Constantinople (Istanbul), Turkey.

ISTANBUL RECONQUERED JOINTLY BY MUSLIM AND CHRISTIANS

The Muslims and the good half of the Christian army conquer Constantinople together, against the enemy Christians. Thereafter, a Christian will say the victory was due to the cross, and the Muslim will say it was due to Islam. A battle between both sides will ensue, and the Muslim Ruler will be martyred.

SYRIA CONQUERED BY CHRISTIANS

The two Christian armies reunite, conquering Syria.

CHRISTIAN DOMINATION

Christians dominate the world up to Khaiber (near Madinah), and they will pursue Muslims with 80 flags, with 12,000 men under each flag.

MUSLIMS AWAIT IMAM MAHDI

TOTAL ECLIPSE

A total eclipse of the sun and moon will occur in Ramadan, prior to Imam Mahdi's emergence.

IMAM MAHDI EMERGES

At age 40, Imam Mahdi appears in Makkah, then flees to Madinah.

The Major Signs (after the emergence of Imam Mahdi)

MUSLIM ARMY MARCHES

The army of Mansoor from Khurasaan will head towards Makkah to aid Imam Mahdi. They will win many battles on the way. No force will be able to stop them. They will carry black flags.

SUFYANI ARMY SWALLOWED BY THE EARTH.

The Sufyaani army (an Anti-Muslim force) from Syria singles out Imam Mahdi for execution. On the way to Makkah, they get swallowed into the ground. A second Sufyani army is created with 960,000 men (of 80 nations).

CONFRONTATION IN SYRIA

Imam Mahdi and the Muslim army go to Syria to confront the Christians. The Christians, before the battle, will ask Muslims for the return of their prisoners-of-war. The Muslims will refuse. The battle will begin. One-third of Imam Mahdi's army will flee (their repentance will not be accepted), one-third will be martyred, and one-third will gain victory over the Christians.

MUSLIM ARMY UNDER IMAM MAHDI CONQUERS PALESTINE JIHAD ON INDIA

A jamaat of Muslims wages Jihad in India and is successful.

SYRIA UNDER MUSLIM RULE

Imam Mahdi returns to Syria and establishes Muslim rule over the lands he passes.

ANIMOSITY RIFE AMONGST THE PEOPLE

At this time, Muslims will be weak and there will be very few pious people.

RUMORS OF EMERGENCE OF DAJJAL

Before the emergence of Dajjal there will be three years of drought. The first year, the skies will retain 1/3 of its water, the second year 2/3, and all of its water the third year.

DAJJAL APPEARS

Dajjal appears. His followers, the Yahudis, 70,000 in number and will wear expensive silk attire and carry double edged swords.

PROPHET ISA(as)APPEARS

Hadhrat Eisa alayhis salaam descends during the lifetime of Imam Mahdi.

DAJJAL KILLED AT THE GATE OF HUDD

Prophet Isa(as) kills Dajjal at the Gate of Hudd, near an Israeli airport, in the valley of "Ifiq." The final war between the Yahudi's will ensue, and the Muslims be victorious.

TOTAL PEACE

With the death of Dajjal, all wars will end. Jihad will be stopped; peace, harmony, and tranquility will be on earth. The earth will produce abundant crops and fruit. The people will follow Islam.

PROPHET ISA(as) RECEIVES REVELATION

The revelation tells that the Yajooj and Majooj will soon be released and the believers should be taken to Mt. Toor (Sinai).

Yajooj And Majooj ("Gog and Magog") Released

The Yajooj and Majooj surge forth in large numbers. They destroy everything in their path in their effort to conquer the world. They will be released in two groups.

YAJOOJ AND MAJOOJ REACH JERUSALEM

When they reach Mount Khamrin in Jerusalem, they will proclaim to have conquered the world. Then they will shoot arrows into the sky to conquer the heavens. The arrows will return blood stained.

HARDSHIPS ON MOUNT TOOR

Scarcity of provisions and hardships will afflict the Muslims. Hadhrat Eisa alayhis salaam and the Muslims will pray for the removal of the calamity.

YAJOOJ AND MAJOOJ KILLED BY INFECTIONS

Their prayers are answered and the Yajooj and Majooj develop boil infections, causing them to burst simultaneously as a result.

EARTH FULL OF STENCH OF CORPSES

Hadhrat Eisa alayhis salaam and his companions pray again and huge birds are sent to pick up the Yajooj and Majooj corpses and dispose of them in Nahbal (according to Tirmidhi), the ocean or elsewhere.

PEACE ON EARTH

It will rain for forty days and the earth will be cleansed. Muslims will burn the bows and arrows of Yajooj and Majooj for 7 years. Life will be peaceful while prophet Isa(as) is alive. The earth will be bountiful. Hadhrat Eisa will live 19 years after marriage.

PROPHET ISA(as) PASSES AWAY AND BURIED NEXT TO MUHAMMED (peace be upon him)

OTHER LEADERS FOLLOW AFTER PROPHET ISA(as)

Jahjaan from Qahtaan, from a tribe in Yemen, will rule as the next Khalifa. Muquad, from a tribe of Banu Tamim will also be a deputy.

SOCIETY SLOWLY DECAYS AND KUFR SETS IN.

THE FINAL SIGNS

THE CAVING IN OF THE GROUND

The ground will cave in: one in the east, one in the west, and one in Hejaz, Saudi Arabia.

THE FORTY DAY SMOKE/FOG

Fog or smoke will cover the skies for forty days. The non-believers will fall unconscious, while Muslims will be ill (develop colds). The skies will then clear up.

THE NIGHT OF THREE NIGHTS

A night three nights long will follow the fog. It will occur in the month of Zil-Hajj after Eid Ul-Adha, and cause much restlessness among the people.

THE RISING OF THE SUN IN THE WEST

After the night of three nights, the following morning the sun will rise in the west. People's repentance will not be accepted after this incident.

THE BEAST FROM THE EARTH APPEARS

On the day later, the Beast from the earth will miraculously emerge from Mount Safaa in Makkah, causing a split in the ground. The beast will be able to talk to people and mark the faces of people, making the believers' faces glitter, and the non-believers' faces darkened.

THE BREEZE FROM THE SOUTH

A breeze from the south causes sores in the armpits of Muslims, which they will die of as a result.

DESTRUCTION OF THE KAABA

The Kaaba will be destroyed by non-Muslim African group. Kufr will be rampant. Haj will be discontinued. The Qur'an will be lifted from the heart of the people, 30 years after the ruler Muquad's death.

FIRE IN YEMEN

The fire will follow people to Syria, after which it will stop.

COMMENCEMENT OF QIYAMAH

Some years after the fire, Qiyaamah begins with the Soor (trumpet) being blown. The year is not known to any person. Qiyaamah will come upon the worst of creation.
　　(source: islaam.org)

CHAPTER VI

Zuhoor-e-Ummat

"It was narrated from Abu Hurairah that the Messenger of Allah (peace be upon him) said: Islam began as something strange and will go back to being strange, so glad tidings to the strangers. (Sunan ibn Majah 3986)"

I have explored the problems in detail but I am only providing an overview of possible solutions because every human is different, and each one of us have different problems and understanding the problem is half the solution.

As I conclude, it is essential to reflect on the responsibilities of a Muslim—both as an individual striving for personal betterment and as a member of a larger community. A true Muslim is someone who sincerely follows the teachings of the Prophet Muhammad (peace be upon him) and the principles of Islam, not just in belief but in action and character.

Being a Muslim means embodying kindness, respect, and good conduct, offering help to those in need, showing gratitude, and practicing patience during hardships. It also involves dealing with people with wisdom and tolerance, maintaining strong moral values, and constantly seeking self-improvement. This journey of self-betterment should be guided by the Qur'an, the Sunnah, and the inspiring lives of the righteous predecessors—the Sahabah and the scholars who dedicated their lives to the service of Allah and humanity.

Ultimately, a good Muslim maintains a deep connection with Allah through sincere worship, regular prayers, supplication, and self-reflection. He continuously seeks forgiveness for their shortcomings, knowing that Allah is Most Merciful and Compassionate. Becoming a better Muslim is a lifelong journey of spiritual growth, self-discipline, and striving to fulfill the purpose of life—serving Allah and benefiting humanity. Here's how we can achieve our Golden age back.

Unity of the Ummah (Oneness)

The strength of the Muslim community lies in its unity.

> "*Narrated An-Nu`man bin Bashir: Allah's Messenger (peace be upon him) said, "You see the believers as regards their being merciful among themselves and showing love among themselves and being kind, resembling one body, so that, if any part of the body is not well then the whole body shares the sleeplessness (insomnia) and fever with it." (Sahih Al Bukhari 6011)*"

We must see each other as brothers and sisters, regardless of nationality, ethnicity, or cultural background. The Five Pillars of Islam, common values, and shared beliefs should bind the Ummah together. Disunity weakens us, while unity makes us stronger against oppression, corruption, and external threats.

Empathy and Mutual Support

Islam emphasizes the importance of brotherhood and solidarity. Every Muslim should support others in times of hardship and joy. This support can be financial, emotional, or simply being present for one another. The more we help each other, the stronger our bond becomes, creating a community where no one is abandoned or left behind.

Strengthening Family Ties

Strong families are the foundation of a strong society. Islam teaches us to respect and care for parents, spouses, children, and relatives. By prioritizing family values and maintaining love, discipline, and faith within households, we can raise righteous future generations who will uphold Islamic principles and contribute positively to society.

Promoting Justice and Equality

The Muslim Ummah must stand for justice and fairness, ensuring that all individuals—regardless of race, gender, or social status—are treated with dignity and respect. The Qur'an commands:

> "*Indeed, Allah commands justice, grace, as well as generosity to close relatives. He forbids indecency, wickedness, and aggression. He instructs you so perhaps you will be mindful.(Qur'an 16:90)*"

Fighting oppression, corruption, and inequality is not only a duty but also a means of bringing barakah (blessings) to the community. A just society thrives, while an unjust one collapses.

Encouraging Education and Knowledge

Knowledge is the greatest weapon of the Ummah. A well-educated Muslim is empowered, wise, and capable of uplifting others. Both religious and secular education are crucial for the progress of the Ummah. Seeking knowledge should not be limited to worldly success, but rather a means of serving Allah and benefiting humanity.

> *"It was narrated from Anas bin Malik that the Messenger of Allah (peace be upon him) said: Seeking knowledge is a duty upon every Muslim, and he who imparts knowledge to those who do not deserve it, is like one who puts a necklace of jewels, pearls and gold around the neck of swines. (Sunan ibn Majah 224)"*

Through education, we can address poverty, ignorance, and injustice, and work towards scientific, economic, and technological advancements while staying true to Islamic principles.

Building Strong Institutions

To strengthen the Ummah, Muslims must establish schools, hospitals, charitable organizations, and social service institutions that cater to the needs of the community. These institutions serve as pillars of social welfare, providing education, healthcare, and financial assistance to those in need.

The early Islamic civilizations thrived because they built centers of learning (madrasas), hospitals (bimaristans), and welfare programs, ensuring that knowledge and support were accessible to all. Reviving this spirit is essential for the modern Ummah.

By focusing on these principles, the Muslim Ummah can restore its strength, unity, and moral integrity, living as a model society guided by the Qur'an and Sunnah. This, in turn, will help Muslims fulfill their responsibilities towards each other and the wider world. Being a good Muslim is not just about personal faith—it is about spreading goodness, standing for justice, and uplifting the community. By committing ourselves to this path, we can revive the lost honor of the Ummah and fulfill our duty as Allah's vicegerents on Earth.

DIY

As a Teenager:

Seek Knowledge: Dedicate time to study the Quran and Hadith to build a strong foundation in Islamic teachings.

Choose Righteous Companions: Surround yourself with friends who encourage you to adhere to Islamic principles and avoid negative influences.

Respect Parents and Elders: Honor and obey your parents, recognizing their sacrifices and seeking their guidance.

Engage in Community Activities: Participate in youth groups or community service to develop a sense of responsibility and belonging.

As a Young Adult:

Maintain Regular Worship: Ensure consistency in daily prayers and other acts of worship, integrating them into your routine.

Pursue Halal Livelihood: Seek education and career opportunities that align with Islamic values, ensuring your earnings are lawful.

Guard Morality: Uphold modesty and chastity, avoiding situations that may lead to temptation or compromise your faith.

Plan for the Future: Consider marriage and family life, preparing yourself to fulfill the responsibilities that come with these roles.

As a Father:

Be a Role Model: Demonstrate Islamic values through your actions, as children emulate their parents.

Provide and Protect: Ensure the family's physical, emotional, and spiritual needs are met, creating a safe and nurturing environment.

Educate Your Children: Teach them about Islam, instilling a love for the faith and guiding them towards righteous living.

Spend Quality Time: Engage in activities that strengthen the bond with your children, fostering open communication and trust.

As a Husband:

Show Kindness and Compassion: Treat your wife with respect and understanding, fulfilling her rights and appreciating her contributions.

Communicate Effectively: Maintain open and honest dialogue to address concerns and strengthen the marital relationship.

Support Her Growth: Encourage your wife's personal and spiritual development, facilitating her pursuits within the bounds of Islam.

Share Responsibilities: Collaborate in managing household duties, recognizing the partnership aspect of marriage.

As a Mother:

Nurture with Love: Provide unconditional love and care, creating a secure environment for your children's growth.

Instill Islamic Values: Teach children about their faith from an early age, incorporating Islamic principles into daily routines.

Be Patient and Understanding: Recognize the challenges children face and offer guidance with empathy and patience.

Maintain Personal Spirituality: Dedicate time for your own spiritual growth, as a strong personal connection with Allah enhances your ability to guide your family.

As an Elder:

Offer Wisdom: Share your life experiences and knowledge to guide younger generations, helping them navigate challenges.

Stay Connected to the Community: Remain active in community affairs, providing support and counsel where needed.

Model Perseverance in Worship: Demonstrate steadfastness in religious practices, inspiring others to remain committed to their faith.

Embrace Humility: Acknowledge the continuous need for personal growth and remain open to learning, regardless of age.

"Abu Umayyah ash-Sha'bani said: I asked AbuTha'labah al-Khushani: What is your opinion about the verse "Care for yourselves". He said: I swear by Allah, I asked the one who was well informed about it; I asked the Messenger of Allah (peace be upon him) it. He said: No, enjoin one another to do what is good and forbid one another to do what is evil. But when you see niggardliness being obeyed, passion being followed, worldly interests being preferred, everyone being charmed with his opinion, then care for yourself, and leave alone what people in general are doing; for ahead of you are days which will require endurance, in which showing endurance will be like grasping live coals. The one who acts rightly during that period will have the reward of fifty men who act as he does. Another version has: He said (The hearers asked:) Messenger of Allah, the reward of fifty of them? He replied: The reward of fifty of you.(Sahaba). (Sunan Abi Dawood 4341)"

"Ma'qil b. Yasar reported Allah's Apostle (peace be upon him) as saying: Worshiping during the period of widespread turmoil is like emigration towards me. (Sahih Muslim 2948a)"

Bonus

These people are 0.2% of the world population yet they are,

65% of American President's Cabinet

90% of Hollywood Film Studio CEOs

83% of the World's Richest Tech company CEOs

55% of American Billionaires

63% top donors to American presidential campaigns

90% of all President's child's spouses

31% of White house staff

75% of NBA team owners

100% of executive leadership at BlackRock

85% of Ad Agency owners

Majority executives at State Street and Vanguard

Run the Federal Reserve.

.

And they have been kicked out of 109 countries namely,

250AD Carthage

325AD Jerusalem

415AD Alexandria

554AD Diocese of Clement(France)

561AD Diocese of Uzes(France)

612AD Visigoth Spain

642AD Visigoth Empire

653AD Toledo

855AD Italy

876AD Sens

1012AD Mayence

1182AD France

1182AD Germany

1276AD Upper Bavaria

1290AD England
1306AD France
1322AD France
1348AD Switzerland
1349AD Heilbronn(Germany)
1349AD Hungary
1388AD Strasbourg
1394AD Germany
1394AD France
1422AD Austria
1424AD Fribourg and Zurich
1426AD Cologne
1432AD Savory
1438AD Mainz
1439AD Augsburg
1453AD Franconia
1453AD Breslau
1454AD Wurzburg
1456AD Bavaria
1485AD Vincenza(Italy)
1492AD Spain
1495AD Lithuania
1497AD Portugal
1499AD Germany
1514AD Strasbourg
1519AD Regensburg
1540AD Naples
1542AD Bohemia
1550AD Genoa
1551AD Bavaria
1555AD Pesaro
1559AD Austria
1561AD Prague

1567AD Wurzburg

1569AD Papal States

1571AD Brandenburg

1582AD Netherlands

1593AD Brunswick

1597AD Cremona, Pavia and Lodi

1614AD Frankfort

1615AD Worms

1619AD Kiev

1649AD Ukraine

1649AD Hamburg

1654AD Little Russia

1656AD Lithuania

1669AD Oran(Africa)

1670AD Vienna

1712AD Sandomir

1727AD Russia

1738AD Wurtemburg

1740AD Little Russia

1744AD Bohemia

1744AD Livonia

1745AD Moravia

1753AD Kovad

1761AD Bordeaux

1772AD Russia

1775AD Warsaw

1789AD Alsace

1804AD Russian Villages

1808AD Russian Countryside

1815AD Lubeck and Bremen

1820AD Bremes

1843AD Austria and Prussia

1862AD United States

1866AD Romania
1919AD Bavaria
(Source; P.E. Grosser & E.G. Halperin, Anti-Semitism: Causes and Effects, New York: Philosophical Library, 1978)

Jazaak Allah

majnūñ ne shahr chhoḌā to sahrā bhī chhoḌ de
nazzāre kī havas ho to lailā bhī chhoḌ de

.

vaa.iz kamāl-e-tark se miltī hai yaañ murād
duniyā jo chhoḌ dī hai to uqbā bhī chhoḌ de

.

taqlīd kī ravish se to behtar hai k͟hud-kushī
rasta bhī DhūñD k͟hizr kā saudā bhī chhoḌ de

.

mānind-e-k͟hāma terī zabāñ par hai harf-e-ġhair
begāna shai pe nāzish-e-bejā bhī chhoḌ de

.

lutf-e-kalām kyā jo na ho dil meñ dard-e-ishq
bismil nahīñ hai tū to taḌapnā bhī chhoḌ de

.

shabnam kī tarah phūloñ pe ro aur chaman se chal
is baaġh meñ qayām kā saudā bhī chhoḌ de

.

hai āshiqī meñ rasm alag sab se baiThnā
but-k͟hāna bhī haram bhī kalīsā bhī chhoḌ de

.

saudā-garī nahīñ ye ibādat k͟hudā kī hai
ai be-k͟habar jazā kī tamannā bhī chhoḌ de

.

achchhā hai dil ke saath rahe pāsbān-e-aql
lekin kabhī kabhī ise tanhā bhī chhoḌ de

.

jiinā vo kyā jo ho nafas-e-ġhair par madār
shohrat kī zindagī kā bharosā bhī chhoḌ de

shoḳhī sī hai savāl-e-mukarrar meñ ai kalīm
shart-e-razā ye hai ki taqāzā bhī chhoḌ de

vaa.iz subūt laa.e jo mai ke javāz meñ
'iqbāl' ko ye zid hai ki piinā bhī chhoḌ de

:)